What others are saying about Cyber Security

"When it comes to cyber-security, Phil is the expert. *Cyber Security: Everything an Executive Needs to Know* is a must read for the C-suite. Phil takes his years of experience in a wide variety of roles and encapsulates the critical lessons he learned into a well-considered approach that even the most seasoned security professionals should read."

~ Malcolm Harkins, Global CISO, Cylance

"Ferraro's transformational approach to IT Security leadership and innovation is unmatched. This book features decades of CISO experience packaged into one resource that provides critical steps you can take as a leader to better prepare your organization from future attacks."

~ Chris Ancharski, Program Director, Evanta

"Phil Ferraro is THE professional I lean on when covering major tech news involving cyber- security. He is extremely knowledgeable and provides great insight into the inner-workings of the cyber-security sector."

~ Mauricio Marin, CBS Las Vegas News Reporter

"Phil Ferraro's no-nonsense guide to cyber security is brought to life with alarming, but real scenarios creating far-reaching business effects. Phil delivers a refreshing and powerful approach to educate business executives and aspiring technology leaders alike, without the typical scare tactics surrounding cyber-security. Readers benefit not only from the perspective of this passionate world-class Global Chief Information Security Officer, but also directly from the voices of outstanding peers across industries to showcase how rock star CISOs approach this challenge."

~ Mike Stango, Director, Security 50

"In our digital age, the issues of cyber security are no longer just for the technology crowd; they matter to us all. In confronting the cyber security problem, it's important for all of us to become knowledgeable and involved. This book makes that possible – and also fascinating. It's everything you need to know about cyber security, wonderfully presented in a clear and smart way."

~ Peggy McColl, New York Times Best Selling Author

CYBER SECURITY:

Everything an Executive Needs to Know

By
Phillip Ferraro

Published by
Hasmark Publishing
judy@hasmarkpublishing.com

Permission should be addressed to: Phil@phillipferraro.com

Editor:
Justin Spizman
www.JustinSpizman.com

Cover Design:
Patti Knoles
www.VirtualGraphicArtsDepartment.com

Layout:
Anne Karklins
annekarklins@gmail.com

ISBN-13: 978-1-988071-20-6
ISBN-10: 1-988071-20-8

This book is dedicated to my parents, Barbara and John Souza. Thank you for always being there for me, and for all your unconditional love, encouragement, and support. Without you both, I would not be where I am.

Acknowledgments

To my wife and best friend Sandra without whose constant support, encouragement, and love this book would not have been written.

To my editor, Justin Spizman, for his constant source of great creative ideas and helpful suggestions for this book, and his ability to teach me how to be a storyteller by putting my thoughts and experiences into words.

To my friend and inspiration Bob Proctor, I thank you for teaching me a much greater understanding of how to overcome and change paradigms and unlock unlimited potential in my life. Your coaching has changed the way I view life.

To Peggy McColl, for amazing training, guidance, and encouragement not only on how to write a book, but also on how to write an international best seller.

I would to like to thank a number of my colleagues – Malcolm Harkins, Bruce Brody, Lou DeSorbo, Scott Goodhart, and Jay Leek – who were incredibly generous with sharing their expert advice and experiences in creating a world class cyber security organization. I am very grateful for them taking the time from their very busy schedules.

I also have been very fortunate to work with so many fantastic people in my long career. Without wanting to make this acknowledgement section longer than the book itself, I want to express my gratitude to my mentors, supervisors, co-workers, team members, and friends who all have contributed to my experiences, which have led to the writing of this book. You know who you are. Thank you!

Table of Contents

Chapter 1: **Are You Next?:** *Assessing Your Internal Risk*   1
   The New Age of Infiltration   1
   The Evolution of the Invisible Thief   2
   A Real Threat   4
   Is My Organization at Risk?   5
   Assessing Your Risk   7
   Building Structure from Within   9
   Cyber-Screwed   10

Chapter 2: **From Top to Bottom:** *It Takes a Village to Prevent a Breach*   15
   Where Does it Begin?   15
   Chief Executive Officer (CEO)   18
   Chief Operating Officer (COO)   18
   Chief Financial Officers (CFO)   19
   Chief Information Officers (CIO)   21
   Managing Risk Management   24
   Human Error   26
   Communicating Your Message   30
   Executing the Action Plan   33
   Security Culture   38

Chapter 3: **Perceived Threats:** *Separating the Real from the Fake*   39
   Understanding the Risk   39
   Anatomy of an Attack   39
   Visualizing the Threat   46
   Fact or Fiction?   55
   Size Really Does Matter   58

Chapter 4: **Damage Done:** *Understanding the Impact of a Breach*   59
   How Deep Does it Go?   59
   Brand and Reputation Damage   59
   Intellectual Property   61
   Class Action Lawsuits   63
   Fines   65
   Damage Done   67
   Can You Be Held Liable for a Breach?   69

Chapter 5: **Protecting Your Business:** *Creating a Rock-Solid Program*   73

    Pre-Planning Your Program   73

    The Hiring Process   80

    Executing the Game Plan   82

    Functional Areas   83

    Business Integration   85

Chapter 6: **Leading the Charge:** *The Role and Responsibilities of a CISO* 87

    Rock Star Qualities   87

    The Responsibilities of a CISO   89

    Security Assessments   90

    Risk Management   91

    Policy and Governance: Auditor Not Implementer   93

    Security Architecture and Engineering   94

    Security Monitoring   95

    Incident Response   96

    Cyber Threat Intelligence   97

        Forensics Investigations   98

        A Day in the Life of a CISO   98

Chapter 7: **Breach Management:** *Recovering from the Carnage*   101

    The Day of Dread   101

    Crisis Action Team   103

    Containment, Mitigation, and Forensics   105

    Recovery and Lessons Learned   107

    The Aftermath   109

Chapter 8: **Cyber Security Roadmap:** *The Path to a Rock Solid Program* 113

    The Cyber Security Roadmap   113

    The Experts Roundtable   119

    A Cyber Farewell   125

About the Author   129

A Letter to the Reader

There was once a time when a business's worst nightmare would be a group of clandestine and hood wearing thieves smashing a window, cracking the safe or cash register, and making away with a pile of hard-earned cash. But times have changed. The threat landscape is significantly different, as well as much more sophisticated and aggressive. Now, and scarier than ever, a well-trained and computer savvy thief can enter your business while you are literally sitting at your desk and obtain extremely sensitive and protected information and, with the click of a few buttons, open the flood gates and release client information, credit card numbers, Intellectual Property, trade secrets, and other content that could cost your company time, effort, and endless amounts of money. The masked bandits have been replaced with calculated and infiltrative computer hackers that can rob you blind while looking you directly in the eye. We call them cyber security thieves.

A cyber security breach can put an organization out of business, or at the very least cost it tens, if not hundreds, of millions of dollars. And that may pale in comparison to the significant damage to brand and reputation. The Board of Directors and the Executive Leaders of the organization are responsible for the success of the business. As such, they should anticipate and be prepared for any future events that could significantly impact the organization. One of those events is a cyber security breach. The Board of Directors and C-Suite Executives face an enormous challenge: a limited understanding of cyber security business risks, the full financial and business impact a breach can have, analyzing and evaluating the right level of investment to protect against these threats, and where and how cyber security should be managed within the organization.

The goal of this book is to help you gain an in depth understanding of each of these significant areas, while learning exactly what steps you, as a leader, can take to properly prepare your organization to face today's constantly evolving threat landscape.

My name is Phil Ferraro, and I am one of the top Chief Information Security Officers (CISO) in the country. For over 15 years as a CISO, I protected and defended organizations against the world's most sophisticated cyber attackers. I give international keynote talks on all aspects of cyber security, and I am one of the few CISOs in the country asked to present on Capitol Hill on cyber security and advanced threats to Senate and Congressional committees. In short, I have seen it all.

While serving as a CISO in the Federal Government, in the Department of Defense, Intelligence Community, and the Federal Communications Commission protecting the nation's most sensitive national security information, I developed and implemented cyber security programs designed to protect and defend against the world's most sophisticated attackers. And I am confident my experience and education can greatly benefit you and your company.

Following nearly 30 years of government service, I served as CISO in Fortune 500 companies developing and building comprehensive global cyber security programs. In October 2014, I was presented with the prestigious Top 10 CISO Breakaway Leader Award that celebrates world-class information security leaders, and honors CISOs and senior security executives whose leadership elevates their people, partners, and business.

Most books on cyber security focus either on technologies or a very speculative high-level approach. The technology approach is written for CISOs and below; the hands-on operators and what technologies they need to implement. The high level approach gives you a 50,000-foot view and then describes the threats to organizations and couches them in great fear, uncertainty, and doubt. Those books do not take the time to provide the level of details needed to understand the overall concept and sensitivities found within cyber security, how it can impact an organization, and what can be done about it right now to ensure your business is protected against future threats.

Since this book is written by a world class Fortune 500 CISO with many years of presenting to and advising Boards of Directors and C-Suite executives, you'll quickly find an inside the trenches approach to handling cyber security breaches before they actually occur. There is clear and concise information that executives need to understand cyber security and develop comprehensive cyber programs. This book will help readers immediately take the information and apply it to their own organizations. Comprehensive cyber programs include a large number of functional areas, and you will find that this book cuts through the fog and provides a clear picture of where and what to focus on to effectively manage cyber business risk.

I am confident that reading this book will be an excellent investment of your time and money. This is one of those books that, after reading it, you will keep close and refer back to often, as you would a reference book. You'll also learn a great deal about the cyber security industry, and exactly how some of the most well-known breaches of information actually occurred. From these stories you will learn valuable lessons that you can then implement into your organization to prevent it from appearing in a scandal on the front-page news.

You will gain a much better understanding of the cyber security threats targeting your business and your industry, why all these big companies are getting breached, and what you can do to significantly lower your risk and raise your security so as not to become a victim. You will also learn what you must do as a senior executive to implement a comprehensive cyber security program, how you can start your plan immediately, what the full impact and financial effects of a breach are and the damage caused to organizations, and you will determine the necessary steps to manage a cyber security crisis. Finally, you will gain access to one of the top cyber security experts in this country who can assist you in developing your strategic plan and goals for protecting your organization.

We now live in a world with cyber-threats around every corner. Even one small data breach can be catastrophic to your business. But preventative maintenance is not nearly as difficult as you think. Investing a little bit of time and money now can be the difference between success and ultimate demise. So together we can overcome the new generation of thieves who can literally rob you blind while wearing their pajamas and sitting in front of their computers.

Chapter 1:

Are You Next?: *Assessing Your Internal Risk*

The New Age of Infiltration

Times have changed. Significantly. For generations and decades before, we were concerned with a man in a hooded sweater throwing a rock through the front window of our business and cleaning out the cash register. But a far more frightening and unexpected threat has replaced the old smash and grab. Now, the most deadly and detrimental action to impact your business can occur at the hands of a guy sitting at his computer in his pajamas half way around the world. Now all it takes is a highly specialized set of skills and an Internet connection to bring your business to its knees. And the worst part: you will never see it coming. There will be no DNA, no fingerprints, and no video of the culprit. This thief will infiltrate your business through the closed circuit back roads of the Internet, leaving no sign of entry or exit. Scary, right?

In 1983, a young computer hacker, while sitting in his bedroom and thinking he was playing a game, almost brought the country to a nuclear World War III with Russia by hacking into the US Department of Defense computer systems.

True story? Actually, this was only the movie War Games. But the scary part is that reality is now mimicking art. The imagination of these writers is now within the realm of the ability of hackers across the world. A simple movie has awakened the senses and pushed countries to create security infrastructure to protect against these potential tragedies.

In 1989, a college student named Robert Morris, son of an NSA computer scientist, wrote a program designed to hack into every computer connected to the fledgling Internet of that time and then replicate itself. This program, now well known as the Morris Worm, nearly took down the entire Internet.

But this was just the start of a huge proliferation of malicious software, known as malware. Antivirus vendors claim that there were over 317 million new pieces of malware created in 2014 alone.

The Evolution of the Invisible Thief

The threat landscape has significantly changed over the past several years. We used to worry about script kiddies, young boys and girls sitting in their bedroom or basement trying to hack into companies just for the challenge and fun of it. They would hack into company websites and deface them, and put images of their hacking name or club on the website simply to gain street (or in this case Internet) cred. The bigger the company you hacked, the more underworld fame you received.

But others, who were more malicious, would create viruses that would spread through companies and across the globe like wildfire. They would send these viruses out in the form of email attachments. Their satisfaction came in watching the total number of infections around the world. The higher the number of infected systems, the greater satisfaction they received. Hackers would compete against one another to create bigger, faster, and stronger viruses. Some would create malicious viruses that would actually delete files. As their abilities developed, they realized that in addition to the fun and excitement of hacking, they could also start profiting by stealing user's personal information for gain. While attempts at these types of things still occur today, even the most basic of security tools in an organization can generally protect against and prevent them from happening, as the methodologies used are now considered very basic. Antivirus and antimalware programs all detect these kinds of attacks… provided your IT administrators keep these systems up to date with the latest signature files.

We have come a long way from the days of script kiddies, web defacements, and basic viruses. What currently keeps executives awake at night is the cyber espionage created by malicious actors. They come in many different varieties and aim at externally attacking organizations through insider information. They are very, very sophisticated, well-funded, and have large teams that work 24 hours a day, 7 days a week, 365 days a year. They simply will not stop until the job is done. In years past, the stealthy attacker would sneak into a network undetected and remain hidden in plain sight all the while siphoning off company data bit by bit.

Unbelievably, a 2013 study showed the median number of days attackers were present on a victim network before they were discovered was 229 days, down from 243 days in 2012.[1] That's seven and a half months of holding information hostage on a company's network while simultaneously stealing intellectual property, trade secrets, Personally Identifiable Information (PII), Payment Card Industry (PCI) or other sensitive, protected, and extremely valuable information. As of the printing of this book, we are still seeing advanced attackers that have been on a victim's network for 6 – 7 months[2] before their discovery. For example, in the case of the recent Target breach the attackers were only on the network for approximately 3-1/2 weeks, yet were able to steal 40 million credit and debit card records and another 70 million records containing PII, a shocking number in and of itself.

More often than not, when an attacker is detected after a lengthy stay on a network, that discovery is made through an external third party, such as the US Federal Bureau of Investigation (FBI), and not the victim organization. These Government agencies are constantly hunting on the Internet or "Dark Web",[3] or are working to detect malicious command and control communications to and from the victims' systems and malicious Internet Protocol locations. In fact, nearly 69% of organizations breached were notified by an outside entity rather than discovering it themselves.[4]

Leading the way in these sophisticated attacks are nation-state attackers, often referred to as Advanced Persistent Threats (APT). Quite often, we hear in the news about state sponsored terrorism. Cyber attacks are just another form of that. Effectively, it is state sponsored cyber terrorism. And don't believe that they only go after government agencies and defense contractors. They target all companies in all industries.

---

1. Mandiant 2014 M-Trends Beyond the Breach Report, https://dl.mandiant.com/EE/library/WP_M-Trends2014_140409.pdf
2. Mandiant 2015 M-Trends: A View from the Front Lines, https://www2.fireeye.com/rs/fireeye/images/rpt-m-trends-2015.pdf
3. The Dark Web is a semi-hidden part of the Internet that requires special software to connect to it. It, and the information it contains, cannot be searched or accessed from normal Internet browsing/connections.
4. Mandiant 2015 M-Trends: A View from the Front Lines, https://www2.fireeye.com/rs/fireeye/images/rpt-m-trends-2015.pdf

Another very capable group of attackers are called Hacktivists. You might have heard of groups with names such as Anonymous, Lulzsec, and others. These groups also target companies in all industries but usually because they disagree with the companies' ideology, policies, or maybe the color of a company logo. There's no rhyme or reason as to who or where they attack.

But remember, there's a big difference between the APTs and the Hacktivists as to how they operate. The APTs will slip in quietly, remain hidden in plain sight, and siphon off intellectual property, trade secrets, sensitive business information, and similar types of data for their own gain; whereas the Hacktivists will breach an organization, find sensitive business data or potentially embarrassing personal information of executives, and then publish that information for the entire world to see.

In later chapters, we will talk more about each of these groups, as well as other groups like organized crime, who like to break in and steal PII, credit card information, and/or Personal Health Information (PHI) to sell on the black market.

A Real Threat

Today the threat of a cyber breach is so high that no organization is safe. The cyber criminals have all the same security technologies that we have, and they use these technologies to develop malware that can evade detection. Although the attackers are very sophisticated with dangerous weapons and tools, a majority of the time they do not use these sophisticated tools because they are unnecessary to breach most organizations. Many companies think they are safe from intrusions by having firewalls, antivirus tools, and intrusion/detection prevention systems that will protect them. But this couldn't be farther from the truth. These security technologies alone are far from capable of stopping a determined attacker. In fact, most companies go so far as to help the attackers. They don't just leave the back door open; they leave the front door wide open with no guard and a big welcome sign flashing over it.

In today's world there are three types of organizations:

    1. Those that have been breached;

2. Those who don't know that they have been breached;

3. Those who don't want to know if they have been breached.

Of these three groups, the ones who have been breached are actually better off. At least they are aware of how bad their security posture is and hopefully have taken the right steps to improve it. As times evolve, so does the amount of damage cyber-security thieves can cause. Those who don't yet know they've been breached are in the most sensitive position, as they have failed to take the proper steps to understand their current risk posture and properly invest in a comprehensive security program. And by comprehensive I don't mean relying on industry best practices, because industry best practices really are not anywhere close to the best. Businesses should go beyond best practices to have a chance of properly defending against real threats. And finally, the third group has their head in the sand. They are of the mindset that "I have never had a heart attack, so I never will." But from past experience, I can tell you that it is not a question of *if* you will be breached, but *when*.

Hacking used to be about the thrill and challenge. Today it is big business and it is growing rapidly. According to the 2015 Verizon Data Breach Investigations Report, there were more than 79,790 security incidents in 2014 alone.[5] This number may be on the low end as not all organizations report being breached.

Do I have your attention yet? If not, let's shine the light on your organization to determine your risk level.

Is My Organization at Risk?

The short answer is yes. In the past few years, the frequency and magnitude of cyber-attacks on organizations has exponentially increased. Boards and C-Suite executives should recognize that cyber attacks are a persistent business risk and an everyday part of doing business in today's world. Cyber attackers are targeting companies both large and small across all industries. To ensure your organization is properly protected, cyber security measures need to be a critical part of the board and CEO's risk oversight

---

5. Verizon Data Breach Investigations Report, http://www.verizonenterprise.com/DBIR/2015/

responsibilities. Yet despite the news we hear every day of major cyber security breaches, there is a gap with many organizations refusing to take the steps to adequately address the organizational risk.

One of the biggest challenges that organizations face in their cyber security risk is with the directors and senior executive's lack of a detailed understanding of what cyber security is, where it should be managed within the organizational structure, and the impact cyber security can have to the bottom line of the organization.

Too many executives see cyber security as an Information Technology (IT) function. One very important point to understand is that cyber security is NOT an IT function! While it is true that the IT Department implements the tools and technologies used to protect and defend the business, everything that cyber security does, or fails to do, can significantly impact the shareholder value of the organization. In short, cyber security is critical to the success of the organization.

The board and the executive leaders of the organization should realize that a comprehensive cyber security program is required to reduce the level of cyber business risk. Without a comprehensive cyber security program, the organization is exposed to a significantly higher level of enterprise and financial risk. The board and C-Suite leadership should have a better understanding of the risk, the legal implications of cyber risk, and the full financial impact a security breach can have on an organization.

Organizations typically have a corporate structure that includes a Chief Operations Officer, a Chief Financial Officer, a Chief Human Resources Officer, Chief Information Officer, and other C-level executives who are experts in their specific fields who contribute to the overall business and success of the organization. Boards and CEOs wouldn't think of building their organizations without having these positions. They are critical to its success and are experts in their respective areas. Cyber security also is critical to the success of the business. The C-level executive and expert responsible for cyber security within an organization is the Chief Information Security Officer (CISO). Yet, so often we see that organizations bury the CISO, if they even have a CISO, two or more levels below where he/she should be in order to be most effective to the business. The CISO role and responsibility is discussed in detail in a later chapter. The CISO should be a peer to the CIO, and they must form a strong partnership in order to be effective.

There are some executives who think that rather than investing in a CISO and a cyber security program, they will just save the money and buy cyber insurance. While cyber insurance is a good idea (we will discuss it in more detail later), it will not prevent a breach nor will it recover all the costs of a breach. Cyber insurance will not help the company one bit with brand and reputation damage. It will not help with shareholder value significantly dropping subsequent to a breach, and it will not reimburse the company for lost revenue. What will help in all these areas is to have an experienced CISO who can build and manage a comprehensive enterprise cyber security program. A good CISO will have a well-trained Incident Response Team who can respond within minutes of detecting a breach to quickly contain it before it becomes serious.

Assessing Your Risk

So with that said, let's take a look at what you need to do to assess the cyber risk of your company.

The Risk Assessment. The first step is conducting a strategic cyber security risk assessment. To this end, it is advantageous for the organization to bring in a 3rd party cyber security consultant who is an expert in cyber security risk frameworks. Ideally this consultant will be a former CISO, and will have the benefit of experience in both the federal government and Fortune 500 organizations. The consultant will base his/her strategic assessment on a proven risk management framework such as the National Institute of Standards and Technology (NIST) Cyber Security Framework. If you are in the Financial Services industry, then they would use a framework like the Federal Financial Institutions Examination Council (FFIEC) Cyber Security Assessment Tool, which is mapped to the NIST security controls. These frameworks provide organizations with a baseline set of industry standards that go beyond best practices for managing cyber security risk. They also assess the organization's legal and regulatory exposure. In a later chapter we will discuss the components of a Request For Proposal (RFP) that you can use to source qualified consultants who can conduct this type of cyber security strategic assessment.

Bringing in an external cyber security consultant to conduct a strategic assessment will determine the organization's overall risk to the business as well as the current security program from a strategic perspective.

Specific areas that should be assessed include, but are not limited to:

- Comparison of your program to an industry-leading program.
- Building a strategic plan to get your program to an industry-leading program.
- Reviewing how security decisions are made, tools are procured, changes are made, and policies are enforced.
- In depth review of network architecture (ingress/egress to/from the network, connections to/from your crown jewels, remote access, network segmentation, and wireless access to networks).
- Review of Payment Card Industry (PCI) infrastructure and Point of Sale (POS) systems.
- Review of applications on the network, dependencies, communications between systems, and vulnerabilities.
- Review Identity and Access Management systems and controls in place, managed and operated.
- In depth review of security architecture from perimeter to endpoint (what tools/ technologies exist, are they sufficient, and what is needed).
- Review IT Compliance programs, tools, and technologies.
- Review policies, SOPs, and training programs.
- Review cyber threat intelligence capability.
- Review Incident Response capability.
- Review network monitoring capability.
- Review cyber organizational structure.

The consultant, or your CISO, should then prepare a Cyber Security Strategic Plan which tells you what needs to be done, how often it needs to be done, and what resources are required. Once this Strategic Plan is prepared, your CISO can then operationalize it and immediately start raising the security profile of the organization while lowering the risk profile. This comprehensive strategic assessment is your first step in determining how at risk your organization is, and what needs to be done to immediately raise your security profile.

Building Structure from Within

To this point, we have discussed a general overview of cyber security threats and the potential carnage they can create within your business. We then discussed assessment tools and evaluating the risk found within your own organization. Now, we will shift our attention to the steps your business leaders can take from the inside out to ensure you are guarded and protected against substantial threats. As with other business risks, cyber security risk must be managed and driven from the top down and at the C-Suite level. To be able to do this effectively, directors and C-Suite executives must have an in-depth, leadership level knowledge of cyber security and exactly how it impacts the business.

Risk is a constant across all organizations. Each business must determine its level of risk appetite, or in other words, the amount of risk the business is willing to accept. With risk comes rewards, but there is a point at which accepting too much risk, particularly cyber risk, becomes dangerous to the business and could result in egregious damage. Some businesses, such as startups, might be willing to accept much more risk than others. The board must determine the level of risk it is willing to accept and also the level of risk tolerance, or variance to the risk appetite. Determining and approving the level of risk is a core function of the board.

Often boards delegate risk oversight to an audit or risk committee; however, these committees often lack the experience, support, or skills necessary to properly understand and address cyber security risk. Often the CIO is asked to provide information on cyber security, but CIOs are technologists responsible for keeping the lights on for all IT systems, applications, and infrastructure, as well as developing new technologies that support the business. They typically are not experts in cyber security, nor do they have the level of hands on experience with cyber security that wouldallow them to expertly advise the board or a risk committee.

Because of the significant impact that a cyber risk can have on shareholder value and the financials of the business, it is advisable that risk oversight is a function of the full board. While the New York Stock Exchange imposes certain risk oversight to audit committees, the rules say that the audit committee is "not the sole body for risk" and that they are to "discuss policies with respect to risk assessment and risk management."[6]

The CEO should make cyber security one of the business's strategic goals and priorities. This needs to be communicated clearly to all leadership, lines of business, and employees throughout the organization. It might require a culture change in the company. This change must start at the top. Make security everyone's responsibility. We will take a closer look at this in the next chapter.

Cyber-Screwed

Still don't believe cyber security is an essential part of any business? Well, wait till you hear what happened to those companies that weren't believers either. There are many reasons why malicious actors conduct cyber espionage. Sometimes the purpose is military or defense related, but more often than not is for commercial gain and profit. They want to steal your intellectual property, trade secrets, and sensitive business information. Rather than spending millions of their own dollars and many years of research and development, they can easily and effortlessly steal the information, and then manufacture the technology cheaper and faster than their competition.

There are several examples of organizations who have gone out of business subsequent to a cyber breach and loss of Intellectual Property, but one of the best known is that of Nortel Networks. Once a Fortune 500 company and North America's largest manufacturer of telephony equipment, they were breached by an Advanced Persistent Threat who remained hidden on

---

6. Section 303A, NYSE Listing Manual

their network for several years and stole their most sensitive data. Hackers working from Chinese IP addresses used seven passwords of Nortel senior executives, including a former CEO, to gain full access to all Nortel networks owned by the company.[7]

In 2004, Nortel's senior IT Security person discovered company data being sent to an Internet Protocol address in China. Further investigation showed that the attacker had been on the network since 2000, or possibly even earlier. Executive management failed to heed the advice of their CISO or provide him the needed cyber security resources. The company took little action to properly protect and secure their networks, data, and most importantly, their Intellectual Property. Executive guidance sent orders down the food chain to simply reset the passwords. For nearly ten years, malicious attackers had access to everything on the Nortel networks. They downloaded research and development data, technical papers, schematics, business plans, corporate executives' email, basically anything they wanted. All they had to do was figure out exactly what they wanted to take.

Interestingly enough, during that time frame a Chinese telecommunications company, Huawei Technologies, with ties to the People's Liberation Army (founder Ren Zhengfei was an engineer in the PLA and Huawei has many contracts with them) grew from a small provider of phone switches and phone products to the world's largest telecommunications equipment provider.

In July of 2000, Nortel's stock hit a peak of $124.50, but by January 2009 it had dropped to 39 cents. After years of losing market share to Chinese companies, the former Fortune 500 Company filed for bankruptcy and is no longer in business.

Nortel remains a good example of a business with its head in the sand, and one that took almost no preventative measures to ensure they were protected. They literally did nothing other than the basic firewalls, intrusion detection systems, and endpoint antivirus. Nortel paid a big price for taking cyber security lightly.

---

7. Gorman, Siobhan (February 14, 2012). "Chinese Hackers Suspected In Long-Term Nortel Breach". *The Wall Street Journal.*

Now let's look at how Kaspersky Labs, a well-established computer security company, was victimized by a sophisticated, very well-planned cyber attack. This company's primary business is research and development of cyber threats and vulnerabilities, as well as having a top selling antivirus/ antimalware suite of security protection tools. In 2015, they were victims of a cyber attack.

If you are wondering how this could have happened, you are not alone. But the bottom line is that these malicious actors are extremely calculated and well-trained. Some people might argue that it wasn't very smart for an Advanced Persistent Threat (APT) to attack a security vendor, as they would have safeguards in place to prevent such a threat. However, these attackers were so confident they would not be detected that they decided to proceed. In fact, they were really interested in learning the latest R&D and new technologies on advanced threat detection from this company. With the knowledge of how a major security company is able to detect malware and threats, they could then develop new malware to avoid detection and allow them to compromise millions of systems around the world.

Following an intensive forensics investigation by Kaspersky, the attackers tracked typical attack protocol by sending spear phishing email to Kaspersky employees located in a smaller office in Asia Pacific.[8] Once they were successful at compromising one or more individual computers, they started their network reconnaissance by mapping out key systems on Kaspersky's networks. At this point they still didn't have to use their sophisticated malware yet, although they did use something known as zero-day exploits. A zero-day is malware that exploits an unknown vulnerability. In other words, the attackers discover a vulnerability in an application, like Adobe or Java, or an operating system, like Microsoft Windows, and then develop malware to exploit it. Because the product manufacturer isn't aware of the vulnerability, there is no patch available for it. Zero-days are readily available to purchase from black market vendors who operate on the Dark Web.[9]

---

8. The Mystery of Duqu 2.0,
   https://cdn.securelist.com/files/2015/06/The_Mystery_of_Duqu_2_0_a_sophisticated_cyberespionage_actor_returns.pdf
9. The Dark Web is a semi-hidden part of the Internet that requires special software to connect to it. It, and the information it contains, cannot be searched or accessed from normal Internet browsing/connections.

From the attacker's perspective, they were able to successfully locate servers that are always up and running. They rarely get rebooted. We all have these servers on our networks. This was important to the attackers because new and sophisticated malware runs in memory. Why is this important? Because most antimalware programs look for malware signatures, known malicious files, and anomalous system behavior (unusual changes or activity on a computer system or hard drive). At the time of the attack, antimalware products did not do a good job of analyzing what was running in memory.

The attackers loaded their malware onto servers, then deleted all traces of how they breached the company. It is not known if Kaspersky ever found the initial entry point into their network. They worked really hard to develop malware that made minimal, if any, changes on the system. This remained under the radar and avoided detection. Most sophisticated malware has something called persistence. When an infected computer is restarted, the malware will also restart. This type of code is usually detectable by a good antimalware program. These attackers developed an ingenious technique for persistence without the need of embedded detectable code.

Had they not attacked a security company, eventually being discovered, this malware would still be in use today, infecting millions of systems around the world. Although the discovery of this malware helps the good guys develop better defensive security technologies and protection, the attackers also generally learn valuable lessons. An early version of this malware was used a few years prior to the second attack. Once discovered, the attackers learned from the information published by security companies, and then redesigned the malware to make it much more sophisticated and undetectable. You can safely bet that they have done the same thing and have something even better today.

The lesson learned here is that even the most security conscious organization can be successfully attacked and breached by determined attackers. You must dedicate resources to developing a rock solid cyber security program that will make your company a hard target. It's not just nation state attackers who are exploiting companies around the world. There are many other groups, who I will describe in detail in later chapters, conducting similar malicious activities. By having a comprehensive cyber security program, and making yourself a hard target, you stand a much better chance of having an attacker move on to a soft target.

The other thing is that you cannot wait. You must take action immediately. Do your strategic cyber security assessment now. Make sure you have a qualified, experienced CISO and provide him/her with the necessary resources to protect, defend, and respond to any cyber threat.

As we have seen, the threat landscape has significantly changed. From small sized companies to large sized enterprises, businesses in all industries are now targets, and are often successfully breached. You cannot afford to maintain the status quo. You must take action, and you must take it immediately. We've seen multiple businesses shut down from a breach, and have witnessed others lose tens to hundreds of millions of dollars for failing to properly protect their business. In the remaining chapters of this book, you will learn what the real vs. perceived threats are, gain a much clearer understanding of the full impact of a cyber breach, learn how to build a cyber security program tailored to your organization, and much more.

Remember, the times of a low-rent thief smashing your window and emptying your cash register are no longer the norm. Now, more than ever, it is the highly trained and tech-savvy generation Y prodigy that is using his/her high-level computer skills to quietly sneak into your business, breach your security, and bring you to your knees. It is now time to exchange your alarm systems and double locked doors for a more advanced and secure security system. One that is based on the changing times and the evolving threats: One that is rooted in cyber security.

Chapter 2:

From Top to Bottom: *It Takes a Village to Prevent a Breach*

Where Does it Begin?

In short, it literally takes a village to prevent a security breach. No one person alone can create or implement the infrastructure to stop a would-be hacker from overwhelming security measures and creating catastrophic carnage to a business and its reputation. The Board of Directors and the Executive Leaders of the organization are responsible for the success of the business. As part of that they must anticipate and be prepared for any future events that could significantly impact the organization. One of those events is a cyber security breach.

In years past, cyber security was of marginal interest to boards and executives. Today it is front and center on their agendas; however, one of the biggest challenges that organizations face in their cyber security risk is with the Board of Directors and C-Suite Executive's lack of understanding of what cyber security is, where it should be managed within the organizational structure, real versus perceived threats, and the impact cyber security can have to the bottom line of the organization. Too much of what is presented to boards and executives is based on fear, uncertainty, and doubt.

As we discussed in Chapter 1, an effective cyber security program starts at the top and trickles down through the organization. First, the board must establish the strategic direction for the company's cyber security program. Many senior executives ask the question: "How do we solve cyber security?" The answer is that cyber security is not a solvable type of issue. It is an ongoing and ever evolving business process. We want our businesses to be as innovative and progressive as possible. We want to provide as much convenience as we can for our customers, as well as our employees. Great advances in technology and science are allowing us to accomplish these things as we incorporate these new technologies. However, with these new technologies come new vulnerabilities along with new attack vectors by criminals. To stay ahead of the attackers is a constant and ongoing battle. For this reason, cyber security must be on the agenda of every board meeting. CEOs must require a regular update from the CISO.

Cyber security responsibility is a new role for directors and executives; one that they feel somewhat uncomfortable with because it's an area of risk with which they are unfamiliar. But armed with the knowledge you will find in this book, you can develop and implement a comprehensive cyber security program that will lower your risk profile considerably.

Think about your organization. Does your board have a member (or members) who maintains an in-depth understanding of cyber security? Do they understand cyber risks and how to properly address them? If not, your board might want to consider adding a well-versed director in cyber security and business risk management to provide a level of expertise currently missing on the board. This might be someone who has previously served as a CISO, or CSO if his/her CSO responsibilities included cyber security. Alternatively, the board might consider contracting with a cyber security expert on an as needed consulting basis, or create an advisory board position, a common practice in today's market.

In regards to cyber security oversight, one of the more important roles for the board is asking the right questions of the CEO and CFO.

The questions the board might ask include:

- *Is our organization currently at risk?* What is our risk versus security profile? The board must be informed of where the company is currently, where they need to be, and the plan of how to get there.

- *Is cyber security risk included in our business risk management framework?* Cyber risk is business risk. The organization must actively pursue mitigating vulnerabilities and liabilities to an acceptable level of risk.

- *Do we have an established cyber security program led by a CISO who has been given the appropriate amount of resources to execute the program?* The CEO must hire and appoint a CISO; preferably he/she is reporting directly to the CEO. The CFO must ensure that the CISO has a cyber security budget sufficient enough to hire the requisite number of staff, or outsource to a Managed Security Services Provider, and purchase leading-edge technology.

- *How are we auditing the cyber security program?* The program should be audited internally on a regular basis, and annually an external consulting firm should conduct a program assessment.

- *Do we have an incident response plan that is tested and trained on regularly?* The incident response plan is one of the most important parts of a comprehensive cyber security program. It must be fully documented including an annex that describes the roles and responsibilities for all senior executives during an actual breach. All executives, or their designees, must be trained regularly on the plan and actions to take during a breach.

- *Do we have a cyber security strategic plan?* The CISO should have and present a strategic plan to the board that outlines the roadmap to proactively protecting the organization from ever-evolving internal and external cyber threats.

- *Do we have a security awareness training program?* This is a team mission. Everyone at all levels of the organization must be aware of cyber threats, and must be properly trained on the do's and don'ts of cyber security.

- *Do we have current security policies in place?* The foundation of the program lies with proper policy development and enforcement of those policies.

- *Do we have cyber insurance?* While cyber insurance won't help with brand or reputation damage following a breach or loss of shareholder value, it can provide reimbursement of many of the costs incurred during a breach.

While the board might have ultimate responsibility for oversight of cyber security, it is a team effort. Everyone at every level in the company has responsibility for cyber security; particularly the senior executives who have responsibilities that directly contribute to the success of your program.

Let's take a look at some of their responsibilities:

Chief Executive Officer (CEO)

There were several very interesting results in a 2015 survey conducted by PwC of 1,322 business leaders across 77 countries.[10] These include:

- CEOs are innovating and accelerating the impact of technology for their customers. CEOs say they are seeing real payoffs from these investments. They expect to take risks to operate within diverse and fluid networks; yet,
- 45% of US CEOs say they are extremely concerned about cyber threats and data security (up 22% from the previous year).
- 62% of this group says that cyber security is strategically very important to their organization.

Tomorrow's CEOs listen closely to their customers, the market, and the world in order to develop and refine their business vision, strategy, and goals to grow their business. They must incorporate cyber security into their strategy and goals to be successful.

Chief Operating Officer (COO)

The COO is another critical member of the organization's cyber security program. The COO must have a more in depth understanding of cyber security than the CEO or board directors might have. As the chief of business operations, the COO must understand how cyber risks can impact business operations. For example, if your company does a large of amount of revenue online, it would be advantageous if the COO understood what a Denial of Service attack is and what steps the CISO is taking to prevent such an attack.

If your organization is in the retail space and has thousands of Point of Sale

---

10. PwC's 18th Annual CEO Survey, 2015, http://www.pwc.com/us/en/ceo-survey/img/ceo-survey-essay-10.pdf

(POS) systems, wouldn't it be good to know how the attackers of Target, Neiman Marcus, Home Depot, and all the others had their POS systems breached and what your CISO is doing to prevent that?

The COO must know what the crown jewels of the organization are and where they are located. If he/she doesn't know, then it makes it extremely difficult to protect them. This could be R&D information that you've spent years and millions of dollars developing, or it could be intellectual property, trade secrets, or maybe just very sensitive business information that gives you a competitive advantage in the market. Direct your business leaders to identify and locate this information and make sure it is provided to the CISO so he/she can properly protect it.

The COO must know where the business is in terms of its cyber security maturity level. It is important to know if a major investment is required immediately, or if you are able to just make incremental updates to add in leading-edge technology to protect against new innovative attack vectors and prevent operational downtime.

Also, the COO must understand the financial and reputation damage that a breach can have on the organization. The COO has oversight of and directs the company's business operations. Often the lines of business leaders will report to the COO. This makes it incumbent on the COO to reinforce regularly to the business leaders the strategic importance of cyber security to the business and to make sure that the business leaders provide their full support to the CISO and the cyber security program. One reason we see so many companies vulnerable to a cyber attack is due to the disconnect between strategy and operations. The COO is in the perfect position to bring these two together. The COO also plays a key role in the event of a cyber security breach. All the roles & responsibilities during a breach are discussed in a later chapter.

Chief Financial Officers (CFO)

Typically, the CFO is not considered a part of the cyber security team; however, CFOs play a significant role in the cyber security of the business. With today's ever-changing threat landscape, the CFO must focus on cyber security and be a strong advocate for making critical investments that will protect the business's most valuable information assets. In addition to all their finance-related responsibilities, CFOs must have a strategic view of their organization's cyber security environment in order to make better, well-informed strategic decisions related to the organization's costs and budget. A major problem in many organizations is that the cyber security program is underfunded. Going back to the faulty thinking that cyber security is an IT function, the cyber security budget often falls under the IT budget. Because it is not the top priority for many CIOs, they fail to allocate the appropriate amount of resources. When times get a little tough, the first budget cut for a CIO is often security. This methodology is a recipe for disaster.

Cyber security should not be under the CIO or in IT in the first place. The CISO should be a peer to the CIO. Regardless of where within the organization cyber security is, it should be its own department with its own budget that is separate from IT's budget. The CISO should be responsible for the P&L of his department. The CISO must be able to understand and plan for CAPEX and OPEX, and build strong business cases for each investment. It is the responsibility of the CFO to establish this financial department and budget for the cyber security program. For general planning for the cyber security program, the CFO can plan on approximately 10 to 14% of the IT budget as the amount needed to fund the cyber security program. This amount could be reduced as the program matures. The cyber security budget will be reviewed and approved in the same manner as any other department, with one exception: These immediate investments need to be a top priority. Waiting any amount of time could result in the organization being breached, as we saw with most of the examples throughout this book, which would result in exponentially higher costs to the business.

The CFO also needs to understand the relevant SEC reporting and regulatory requirements relating to cyber security, and ensure the CISO has that same level of understanding and implements compliance to them in the cyber security program. It is important to review these policies closely, as the more costly breaches there are globally, the more exclusions insurance companies are going to put in into the policy.

Today's top CFOs save their organizations the embarrassment and financial impact of a breach by taking proactive steps to build a comprehensive cyber security program. The CFO is in a perfect position to advocate for necessary investments and provide the required resources that will assist the CISO in preventing a breach.

Chief Information Officers (CIO)

The debate on whether or not the CISO should report to the CIO or another C-Suite executive has been ongoing for years. Both sides will argue the pros and cons based on their personal experience or agendas. CIOs are getting fired due to major security breaches like we saw with Target. Part of Target's problem was that they didn't even have a CISO before being breached. Some might argue that the level of security does not go up or down significantly whether or not the CISO reports to the CIO or another executive. Rather than debate personal preference, let's look at empirical evidence that proves that having the CISO report to an executive outside of IT actually does improve the organization's security when measured against downtime and financial losses.

The 2014 Ponemon Global State of Information Security Survey[11] states:

- With more than 9,000 respondents from around the globe, the survey found that those organizations in which the CISO reported to the CIO experienced **14% more downtime** due to cyber security incidents than those organizations in which the CISO reported to the CEO.
- And, when the CISO reported to the CIO, **financial losses were 46% higher** than when the CISO reported to the CEO. In fact, having the CISO report to almost any position in senior management other than the CIO (Board of Directors, CFO, etc.) reduced financial losses from cyber incidents.

It can be said that the transformation of the CISO role in today's world is similar to that of the CIO some 30 years ago. At that time, as organizations

---

11. 2014 Ponemon Global State of Information Security Survey, http://www.pwchk.com/home/eng/rcs_info_security_2014.html

were adding in more and more technology, they created a CIO role. Unfortunately, they buried the CIO under business operations teams. Over time, as senior corporate executives realized the importance of the CIO's role to the business, the position was elevated to the current point where many CIOs now report directly to the CEO, or in some cases the COO or CFO. You do not have the luxury of time to watch the CISO role prove its importance to the success of the business.

In 2012, foreign hackers breached the State of South Carolina's Department of Revenue and stole nearly 4 million social security numbers and 400,000 credit and debit card numbers. Subsequent to the breach, in October 2012, Governor Mikki R. Haley issued an Executive Order directing the state's Inspector General to conduct an investigation not into the breach itself, as federal law enforcement was investigating that, but into how the state currently performed cyber security and to determine a way forward to improve it.

In addition to internal state sources, the IG's review also included interviews with experts from the private sector, the National Association of State CIOs, Multi-State Information Sharing and Analysis Center, Gartner, Deloitte, CISCO, University of South Carolina, and Clemson; CIOs and officials from six other states, including three states with experience in significant data losses; and cyber security literature from a variety of sources including, but not limited to, CERT-Carnegie Mellon, Sans Institute, and Information Security Audit and Control Association.

In the IG's report[12] they indicated that cyber security tasks were being performed daily. Cyber security was, like many government organizations, under the CIO. The state IT Solutions Committee, which included CIOs of 18 agencies, agreed "There was a sense agencies were conducting mission critical INFOSEC [cyber security], but had little capacity to be proactive in an increasing threat and vulnerability environment."

---

12. State Government Information Security Initiative: Current Situation and a Way Forward, http://ef67fc04ce9b132c2b32-8aedd782b7d22cfe0d1146da69a52436.r14.cf1.rackcdn.com/south-carolina-inspector-general-centralize-security-ere-source-1-a-5336.pdf

The IG made six recommendations, which were subsequently accepted and implemented:

- Establish a comprehensive cyber security program;
- Establish a CISO position outside of IT to lead the development and implementation of a statewide comprehensive cyber security program;
- Establish a federated governance model – cyber security authority resting with the CISO to establish the program and policies and then delegate authority, as needed, to meet operational requirements, but still subject to oversight and audit;
- Designate a leader to take responsibility for proactively driving statewide cyber security issues while they created the new state CISO position and hired a new CISO into it;
- Establish a steering committee to expedite and provide oversight of the development of a statewide comprehensive cyber security program;
- Hire a consultant to assist in building the governance framework and in developing statewide cyber security implementation options.

If we look at this example, we see they have successfully changed their model to make the CIO and CISO peers who report to a COO, and together they have successfully built a solid cyber security program that has not been compromised since the remodel.

As you can see, the CIO's role in cyber security is still a critical one. The CIO and the CISO are partners. They must build a very good rapport and work closely together to make sure security and IT are aligned with the company's business objectives as well as the risk appetite. This is best accomplished when they are peers and have an equal say in the discussion. The CIO must make cyber security a top priority and communicate that throughout his/her entire IT organization. He/she must direct their staff to work closely with the cyber security teams.

The CIO's teams are the implementers of security functions, whereas the CISO's teams provide the governance, oversight, and direction of what security controls need to be implemented. For example, the CIO's network engineers will manage the firewalls, but it will be the CISO's security engineers who will approve any changes made to the firewalls. This is one example of how the security and IT check and balance system should work within an organization.

The CIO will make sure that the IT developers and project managers include cyber security in all projects from the beginning of said projects in order to ensure that security can be built in rather than bolted on afterwards. Bringing in cyber security early on provides more accurate project timelines and budgets.

Managing Risk Management

Now that we have described the roles of the executives in relation to cyber security, let's consider the best practices for executives in relation to the overall process of risk management. Some of these include:

- *Incorporate cyber security risk management into existing business risk management processes.* Cyber security should not be considered a compliance checklist. The same approach taken for other business risk must be taken with cyber security. The same due diligence must be applied. Your CISO must work closely with your Chief Risk Officer, or equivalent executive responsible for overseeing and managing business risk to an acceptable level.

- *Cyber security risk management decisions should be regularly communicated to the CEO and the board.* The CEO should be actively engaged in defining the cyber security risk strategy and acceptable levels of risk. This strategy enables more cost effective management of the risks. It also aligns cyber security risks with the business needs of the organization. There should be regular communication between the CEO and the CISO. The CISO is responsible for keeping the CEO aware of current risks affecting their organization, as well as any associated business impact. The CISO also will report to the board at each quarterly board meeting.

- *The cyber security program must exceed industry best practices in all aspects of the program.* A comprehensive cyber security program begins with implementing baseline standards such as the National Institute of Standards and Technology (NIST) Cyber Security Risk

Management Framework. By leveraging and implementing a proven framework, you provide the starting point in building an all-inclusive program to protect systems and detect potential problems. It will help to create the processes that will keep your cyber security teams informed of current threats and enable timely incident response and recovery. Using traditional "best practices" to address known vulnerabilities relies on legacy processes and procedures, and does not adequately address new and dynamic threats, or counter sophisticated adversaries. This is why your CISO must implement leading-edge technologies and be extremely vigilant about keeping these technologies up-to-date. Your CISO should be visionary and think outside the box. Many of the new cutting edge technologies allow you to do more with less, making it more cost efficient to the business. Leading-edge technologies also allow your employees to be more productive and innovative, as the technologies are designed to know what is happening on your networks rather than relying on locking down all the users.

- *Ensure you have a detailed cyber security incident response program that includes crisis action planning.* No matter how much you invest in cyber security people, processes, and technology, there is always a strong possibility that a determined attacker can breach your organization. That's not saying you should reduce your cyber security spending. Absolutely not! You want to make your organization as much of a hard target as you can, so the attacker will move on to a softer target. But keep in mind that it only takes one single employee, whether yours or from a 3rd party vendor or partner, to create an opening for an attacker to get in. Therefore, it is extremely important to have a well-developed incident response plan. This plan outlines the processes your cyber security team uses for any security incident. It provides an escalation process depending on the severity of the incident. It also contains an annex with the roles, responsibilities, actions, and management considerations for the C-Suite during a breach. This concept is so important I have dedicated an entire chapter in this book to discussing it in much more detail.

With the roles and responsibilities clearly defined, and an overall process in place for cyber risk management, it puts us in a much better position for creating an effective cyber security program and preventing a breach. However, there is one major portion of our village that we have not yet addressed – our users.

Human Error

Regardless of the role you play, and the implementables you create regarding risk management, in reality any business will always remain susceptible to human error. Ask any cyber security professional what the number one weakness is within an organization and they will tell you it is the end users. We can deploy millions of dollars of security technologies, but it only takes one user, either knowingly or unknowingly, to open a door and allow an attacker in.

An IBM cyber security intelligence report[13] indicates that over 95% of all security incidents that were investigated show human error as a contributing factor. These include IT personnel not patching systems or using default passwords, or users having weak passwords, but the most prevalent factor is users opening malware infected attachments in email or clicking on links in email that go to compromised or malicious websites. Attackers also use social engineering techniques to gain entry into organization's networks. These techniques can include the use of friending, following or connecting to targeted users on social media sites like Facebook, Twitter, LinkedIn, and the like. Once connected, they then obtain the business email of the users and send phishing email to them. Or, sometimes they know that users will connect to the social media websites during the day from work. The attackers can send malicious files to the user through these sites with the hope that they will download the file at work. Another technique of social engineering is going to the business location. They can hang out around the doors, or in authorized smoking areas outside the building, then piggy back (follow the users back inside the building) without having to show ID or swipe a badge, and then find an open office and get onto the

---

13. http://www.slideshare.net/ibmsecurity/2014-cyber-security-intelligence-index?from_action=save

network. Yet another form of social engineering is malicious actors calling users and saying that they are from the IT Help Desk and there is a problem with their account. They need their username and password to reset the account and fix the problem.

These are just a few of the reasons why it is so important to not only conduct regular security awareness training and education, but also to develop a culture of security in the organization. This, too, starts at the top and runs down through all levels of management. Managers at all levels must constantly remind their users to be vigilant and practice good security. This does not mean that users will be "locked down" in their activities. In fact, just the opposite. A good CISO will be innovative and put technologies in place that will allow users to be more productive by allowing them to do everything they need to do for their work, but will have tools and technologies that monitor all activities on the networks. The CISO should run spear phishing tests. For all those users who click on a link and provide credentials, they will need to go through retraining. Monthly cyber newsletters that include ways users can protect themselves at home, on social media, prevent Internet child bullying, and similar topics will get the users reading, learning and practicing good security habits. Over time the security culture will begin to change, which will help in raising the security posture of the organization.

If we look at our recent history, we can easily find dozens of major catastrophes that have happened due to human error. One horrific example that could have been avoided happened on February 1, 2003. As the Space Shuttle Columbia (STS-107) began to re-enter the earth's atmosphere, damage to the thermal protection system on the left wing that occurred during takeoff exposed the shuttle to intensive levels of heat. The shuttle's frame started melting and then literally disintegrated during reentry. Sadly, all seven crewmembers perished. The worst part about this event is that the both the threat (intensive heat on reentry) and the vulnerability (problems with the foam insulation and the thermal protection system) were known and could have been properly addressed to prevent this event.

The Columbia's mission was to fly up to the International Space Station to assist with its construction and development. During takeoff and exiting of the earth's atmosphere, NASA personnel observing all aspects of the mission noticed that a section of thermal insulation broke off and hit the left wing of the shuttle damaging the leading-edge. After some discussion in the NASA ground station, they decided not to tell the Columbia's crew, as the NASA managers felt that the crew probably could not fix the issue while in space. NASA knew about this problem with insulation panels for years, yet they failed to have a contingency plan to fix the issue if it occurred during a flight. Unbelievably, they literally kept their fingers crossed and hoped that the Columbia would be OK during reentry.

Following the disaster, the government established the Columbia Accident Investigation Board,[14] to conduct an independent investigation into the events leading up to the flight, and the processes and procedures used by NASA, to determine if this could have been prevented. After seven months of investigation, the board concluded that NASA's organizational structure and processes were seriously flawed.

The organizational causes of this accident included:
- The program's history and culture, including the original compromises that were required to gain approval for the Shuttle
- Subsequent years of resource constraints
- Fluctuating priorities
- Schedule pressures
- Lack of an agreed upon national vision for human space flight

Additionally, there were cultural traits and organizational practices detrimental to safety that were allowed to develop, including:
- Reliance on past success as a substitute for sound engineering practices
- Organizational barriers that prevented effective communication of critical safety information
- Stifled professional differences of opinion
- Lack of integrated management across program elements

---

14. Columbia Accident Investigation Board Report, http://www.nasa.gov/columbia/home/CAIB_Vol1.html

- The evolution of an informal chain of command and decision-making processes that operated outside the organization's rules

The board also concluded that, although very risky, the crew could have conducted a spacewalk repair or a separate rescue mission if NASA acted quickly enough, either of which might have saved the crew and prevented this disaster.

If you were wondering why I am discussing a space disaster in a book on cyber security, the answer, I hope, would be obvious. You could change the Columbia's name to the name of your organization. Change the mission to your company's mission. The disaster, which could have been avoided, is a major cyber security breach of your business, one that you, too, can avoid. How can you avoid this? Take a look back at the findings of the Columbia accident. As I read through them, it sounds exactly like what is happening in organizations around the world that are failing at cyber security.

Let's look briefly at each one and put them into cyber security related concerns that must be addressed:

Organizational issues:

- Do you have a cyber security program? Is it at the right operational level in the company? What is your security culture? What is the approval process for cyber security decisions?
- Does your cyber security program suffer from years of resource constraints?
- Is cyber a high priority in the business or does it suffer from fluctuating priorities?
- Does cyber security take a back seat at times to IT or other operational schedule pressures?
- Is there a lack of an agreed upon cyber security vision at the board and senior executive levels?

Cultural traits and organizational practices detrimental to cyber security:

- Are you relying on past success of never being breached as a substitute for having a sound cyber program?

- Are organizational barriers preventing effective communication, at all levels, of cyber security priority and importance?

- Are there stifled professional differences of opinion as to where cyber security should be in the organization and how it is implemented?

- Is there a lack of integrated cyber security management and a shortage of skilled cyber staff across business elements?

- Is there an ineffective chain of command and decision-making processes on cyber security decisions that impact the business?

As you can see, the similarities are uncanny. Don't let human error and poor decision-making in your organization make you the next cyber security disaster. You must implement a comprehensive program today. The hackers and cyber criminals are not waiting. They are attacking your company as you are reading this. Take action now.

Communicating Your Message

We all agree it is a team game, but how do you create and then implement a substantive and consistent message that reaches all corners of a business? Too many executives see cyber security as an Information Technology (IT) function. As we have said a number of times, it is not. Cyber security is a business function. While it is true that the IT Department implements the tools and technologies that are used to protect and defend the business, everything that cyber security does, or fails to do, can considerably impact the shareholder value of the organization. Cyber security is critical to the success of the organization. Leadership must establish an enterprise-wide cyber risk management framework with adequate staffing and budget. Boards and executives must take an active role in making sure the organization has a comprehensive cyber security organization and program, or at a minimum, ensure that the cyber security is outsourced to a reputable Managed Security Service Provider who can provide and manage all aspects of a comprehensive cyber security program.

In today's world of ever-changing sophisticated cyber threats, it is quite important that organizations establish a culture of responsibility; a new and improved security culture. Everyone in the organization must work together to maintain vigilant practices that reduce cyber risk. Regardless of the amount of money corporations invest into their security tools and technologies in order to keep malicious actors out and prevent a breach, these efforts often fall short.

Now that we clearly understand that a comprehensive cyber security program is a must and is a team mission, we must now think about how we communicate this message throughout the organization. How will we implement this new security culture? It starts at the top with the most visible and well-known person in the organization – the CEO.

Depending on the type of business that you are in, the CEO may consider adding one or two words to the vision or mission statements that include security. For example, let's look at the vision statement of a Fortune 500 pharmaceutical company, Pfizer: "We will be recognized for meeting the diverse medical needs of patients in Emerging Markets around the world in an innovative, socially responsible and commercially viable manner."

What if a hacker was to breach the organization and modify the formula or the manufacturing process for one or more of their products, which are designed to help people, and then change the formula or manufacturing process into something that is potentially harmful or deadly? Can we modify the vision statement to include cyber security? Absolutely! What if we added one word to the statement and made it: "We will be recognized for meeting the diverse medical needs of patients in Emerging Markets around the world in a *secure*, innovative, socially responsible and commercially viable manner." Now we have made it clear that this company is focused on protecting its customers and products from any harm.

Here's another example in the financial services industry. Let's say their mission statement currently states, "To become the most respected provider of financial transaction services." Similarly, like the previous example, make a small change to say, "To become the most respected provider of *secure* financial transaction services." This small change now indicates to all that security and providing secure services is a core value and function for this company.

In order for you to develop a successful security culture, security issues must be considered as part of your business's operations and decision-making processes.

From the vision, we include cyber security in the mission statement, and then the strategic goals. This not only sends a clear message to everyone in the organization, but also to customers, business partners, regulators, merchants, and so on. In fact, clearly stating the importance of security will enhance your brand and reputation, particularly in view of all the big name breaches we have seen over the past several years.

As business leaders and managers start incorporating security into their goals and objectives, employees will also start becoming more aware. The CISO's approach is a little bit different. The CISO has to make sure that everything done in the cyber security program is in line with the business strategy. So the business incorporates cyber security, and cyber security aligns with the business. It is a synergistic partnership to secure the company and its information and systems.

Here's the bottom line on security culture – your organization will have a much greater chance of protecting your intellectual property, trade secrets, sensitive business and customer information if, and only if, every member of the team plays an active part. All employees, regardless of their position in the company, need to understand how security relates to them. The last thing you want is for your employees to dismiss cyber security as somebody else's problem.

Even with updating the vision and mission statements, and adding in security goals and objectives, the organization must create an effective security awareness training program. A lack of security awareness in the business could cause a gap in the company's implementation of cyber security. Your organization must ensure that employees are properly trained and aware of their responsibility in securing sensitive business and customer information assets.

Your CISO will create a cyber security awareness and training program. In addition to a mandatory annual training program that is required of all users, the same as you would ethics training or any other mandatory compliance training, the CISO will send out monthly cyber awareness newsletters as described earlier in this chapter. He/she will also create a much more in depth education program specifically for employees who have significant cyber security responsibilities such as team members in cyber security, IT, and others like DBAs, data owners, and program managers.

Look at companies in the financial services industry, or aerospace & defense companies with classified government contracts. These are some of the most heavily targeted companies in the world, but the amount of successful breaches due to human error is significantly lower than other industries because they have created and successfully implemented very strong security cultures. Ask any of their employees if security is important to their company and you will hear a resounding YES!

But it's not just in government and financial services. When you set the tone for the culture at the top, it permeates throughout the entire organization. In December 2013, the State of Kansas legislature directed the State to contract for a comprehensive security audit[15] of the State Lottery. The results indicated a very strong security culture within the organization. The interviewed employees "believe that management sets a strong tone on the importance of security and believe that security measures are consistently applied throughout the organization. Every Kansas Lottery employee supports the Lottery's security program."

Examples like these should be the goal for all organizations.

Executing the Action Plan

At each level, your team will need direction. It is easy to create a game plan and then disseminate that plan to the masses. But the activation can be quite difficult. How can you create clear-cut responsibilities and align them with a checks and balance system to ensure that the head knows what the tail is doing? We must implement the right measures to ensure that all parts of the armor are built and maintained. Even a small area of weakness can be open season for a seasoned hacker. So with that

---

15. Security Audit of the Kansas Lottery, Final Public Report, http://www.kslpa.org/assets/files/reports/R-14-001.pdf

said, there should be clarity surrounding each and every role and the accompanying responsibilities.

We have defined the roles and responsibilities for several key positions in the organization. We have developed a security awareness training program to get the word out and raise awareness levels. Next we need to actually get our employees to execute that guidance.

Consider the answers to questions like:

- *How do you link your new cyber security strategic objectives with actual employee performance?*
- *How do you get your executives, managers, and employees to actually care about and perform security?*
- *What is one of the most important parts of their position with your company? Their compensation.*
- *Do you want to get their attention quickly? Then implement security performance objectives and measures that are linked to their annual bonuses and promotions.*

Cyber security performance measures provide a way for you to monitor and ensure that your organization's cyber security controls and program are being supported and properly implemented. Using performance measures also helps you to assess the effectiveness of the cyber security controls that are being used to protect the company and its crown jewels.

In order to demonstrate the importance of cyber security within your business, at least one cyber security goal or objective should be required for each employee. As you would with any other performance goals, these are reviewed at least quarterly with each employee. You can develop cyber security performance measures at every level within your organization.

As CEO, I would have a dialogue with my executives that would sound something like this: "Team, as we lead this company to become the market leader in our industry, one thing we must make a top priority is that we do not allow ourselves to have a lapse in security that results in a major cyber security breach. To that end, I will be adding one new performance objective for each of you that is related to establishing and supporting cyber security as a top priority for this organization. I expect that each of you, in your area of expertise, will do everything within your authority to support our cyber security program. My level of measure will be two-fold. First, not being breached, and second, direct feedback from the CISO. In turn, I want each of you to do the same with all of your managers and employees. HR, I am tasking you with oversight of this project to make sure that we have updated goals and objectives for every employee."

Within your cyber security department and within the IT department, there would be multiple security performance objectives in support of the organization's cyber security program and the business's strategic objectives and mission.

Security awareness and training are essential components in creating a security culture within your organization. As a leader in your company, it is important that you have an understanding of the challenges of creating a new culture, and how security training and awareness can help. One methodology is to approach the culture change the same way you would for any other major change. Dust off any of your good change management books, or just keep reading here for the right approach. Here is a list of the steps you can take to make the change:

1. ***Make your employees aware of the need for the change***. Decide how you are going to start communicating to them that it is critical to the long-term success of the organization to raise the security posture and lower the risk levels. Just give them a taste that change is coming.

2. ***Involve those affected by the change, in the change process***. While it might not be feasible to have open dialogues with thousands of employees, you could conduct a survey, or have an open blog on an Intranet page, or any of many other possibilities that let your employees know that their input to the change is welcome. Those who feel that they are part of the process are more willing to accept the change.

3. ***Provide notification of the proposed changes***. That you might be hiring a new CISO, expanding the cyber security department,

implementing mandatory annual cyber security training, requiring employee ID badges to be worn and visible above the waist, implementing new performance objectives that include a cyber security objective, or whatever the specific changes will be.

4. ***Welcome a period of feedback.*** At the end of this, consider the feedback, make changes if appropriate, and then start implementing the changes.

5. ***Incorporate as an ongoing process to ensure success of the program.*** Cyber security is not a fire and forget type of activity. Once changes are implemented, you must constantly review the new processes and procedures. Cyber threats are constantly evolving, so your processes must constantly change in order to meet the new threats.

There is not a 'one size fits all' solution, so you will need to develop a solution that fits best for your business. If you do not provide your staff with the appropriate details and guidance, then you cannot be surprised if you find them doing things incorrectly, or more importantly in a manner that puts the organization at risk.

Similarly, the program will not be successful if the team members that you hire for your cyber security department do not have the right skills and personality. A major challenge for organizations, and CISOs in particular, is in hiring quality cyber security personnel. With today's ever evolving cyber threats and more and more organizations realizing they need to step up their cyber programs, the demand for cyber security personnel far exceeds the supply. This paradigm is not expected to change in the near future.

The skillset required of a cyber security professional requires much more specialized experience than typical IT employees have. IT technicians typically work on a few systems that do not change dramatically, and if one of those systems has an issue, there usually is a backup system, or that system can be back up and running quickly. With cyber security experts, the threats, vulnerabilities, and attack vectors are constantly changing. If a breach occurs, it is much more than just a technical issue or a business continuity issue. It affects all aspects of the business, all employees, customers, merchants, regulators, and other stakeholders.

When hiring cyber security experts, there typically are a few characteristics that you should look for – these include:

1. Experience. They must have the requisite cyber security experience for the position you are hiring. Cyber security is quite a broad field with many specialty areas. For example, there are cyber threat analyses, forensics investigations, malware reverse engineering, cyber threat intelligence, security architecture & engineering, and some of the less technical areas such as policy, training, compliance and governance. You do not need personnel who are experienced in all areas, but ideally they are experienced in two or more.

2. Personality. In addition to the technical skills, the personal side is equally as important. You can train staff in new technical skills, but you can't teach them new personality traits. You want team members who are passionate about cyber security and leading-edge technology. These are your real "geek squad" team members. They eat, breathe, and live cyber. They love the fact that the cyber environment is constantly changing. They are very inquisitive and suspicious of little things they see on the network. They dig down deep and find the little indicators that actually could be indicators of compromise. They often have home networks that they attack, and they test new tools and technologies. They do whatever is needed to find solutions to issues.

3. Flexibility. They also tend to think outside the box, so encouraging that behavior while supporting idea generation helps to build a great team. It is better to try new ideas and fail, while learning from and gaining valuable experience, than not trying at all. One thing to keep in mind is that these types thrive in a very non-traditional work environment. They prefer to work on teams where there is a relaxed dress code, flexible hours, and the ability to test new technologies and stay current on their skills. They also don't seek a traditional career path. They might prefer a lateral move cross training into another cyber field rather than upward mobility.

As difficult as it is to recruit cyber experts, you must be prepared to pay higher wages for this level of expertise, as well as authorizing relocation assistance. If your compensation levels are middle of the road, what HR likes to classify as "competitive," or worse, are low, then expect a high turnover rate, if you can hire quality people at all. Depending on where your office is physically located, you might not have a deep pool from which to hire. If you are in a major metropolitan area, then the relocation assistance might not be necessary.

4. Retention. Remember, you must have a plan for retention. If you establish a non-traditional work environment, at least for your cyber security team, that's a good start. You must also budget for annual training for these personnel so that they can keep their skills sharp and obtain industry certifications. Additionally, they should be able to attend at least one job related security conference per year. These are all factors to include when preparing the annual cyber security budget.

Leading this operation is your CISO. This role is so critical to the organization that I have dedicated an entire chapter to it later in the book.

Security Culture

As you can see, it takes an entire village to prevent a breach and keep your organization safe. From the boardroom, to the senior executives, down to every employee, and in particular your cyber security team, everyone has an important role in the security of the organization. Because of the ever changing threat landscape and the new technologies being developed regularly to combat the threats, every level must participate collaboratively and understand their specific role and responsibilities to keep your business safe. An effective cyber security program starts with the board's oversight and guidance. This is made a high priority by the CEO and then promulgated throughout the organization. This is followed by the CISO's development and implementation of strategic and tactical plans and operations in line with business objectives, and includes training and education of all employees.

In the next chapter we discuss perceived threats and separate the real from the myths.

Chapter 3:

Perceived Threats: *Separating the Real from the Fake*

Understanding the Risk

Many C-level executives and Board Directors often wonder who would attack them and for what reason. They often think that their organization is too small to be a target, or that they are in an industry that wouldn't be of much interest to a potential attacker. But the truth is that no company is immune from cyber-attacks. It is important to obtain a strong understanding of who your cyber enemy is, especially if you are going to be able to defend against them. Large organizations ($1B in revenue and above) are better at detecting incidents, since they generally dedicate more resources into their cyber programs. However, they are a treasure trove of information that malicious attackers constantly choose to attack. Attackers frequently target mid-sized organizations ($100M in revenue and above), as they know that these companies often do not provide adequate security resources nor do they have comprehensive cyber programs. Small sized organizations are frequently targeted as they make little investment at all in cyber security, and so can be used as pivot points for attackers to move into the mid- and large sized companies, as we saw in the Target breach.

Let's take a look at the specific attack vectors and the likelihood of a potential attack in small, medium, and large enterprise size organizations. Having a better understanding of the scope of threat in each of these different areas will give you more knowledge of the reality of what could occur in your size company, and the attack methods often used to gain entry and control of these organizations.

Anatomy of an attack

There are many different attack vectors through which a potential attacker can impact your business. They have the sophistication, tools, and technologies to hack through firewalls and websites, but normally do not have to use those skills because there are much easier and much quieter ways to breach an organization. Let's take an in depth look at how attackers breach companies and why it is so difficult for your cyber security teams to prevent these breaches.

Large Enterprise Organizations

Attackers know that large enterprises typically have much better cyber security than medium and small size companies, and therefore need to use a different approach in their attacks. Attackers are very good at doing their homework, or more accurately, their reconnaissance of their target organization. They will start with your company's public websites. They will search all Social Media sites, both at an organizational as well as an individual employee level. They will do in-depth Google searches on the company, its employees, and employee family members to gather up every bit of information that might allow them to find a crack in the armor.

The Attack:

They will search for and record any information that might help them in their attack, such as names, email addresses, phone numbers, locations, or key personnel in the company. It is strongly recommended, if at all possible, not to publicly post the email addresses or direct phone numbers of individuals. Instead post the main information number of the company. If email addresses are posted, then these employees could be victims of a spear phishing attack; for senior executives the term is whale phishing.

Spear or whale phishing is where the attacker sends a targeted email directly to an individual, rather than sending to a large group of employees and hoping one will respond. The attackers can be very crafty. From their Internet reconnaissance they can often find the names of senior company personnel. They create an email account using the name of one of these persons in a popular program like Gmail, Yahoo, Hotmail, etc. For the subject of the email, they will put something very topical and recently in the news about the company. For example, a subject line might read: "Our company just won a new multimillion-dollar contract." Next, they create and send the email individually to multiple people in the company.

There will be a short personalized note in the body of the email and a link that looks like it goes to a valid business website. In fact, it will be a valid business website, but the attacker will have previously compromised one of the site's web pages and uploaded malware to that page.

This is a security professional's nightmare. The attacker, and your cyber security team, know that at least one recipient will click on the link. So far, the attack bypassed all the security tools you may have. But wait, you say security tells you that you have really good antivirus and antimalware on every system, so that'll catch it, right? Wrong! Or maybe the employee won't click on or mouse over anything on the website, so you're safe, right? Wrong again!

Here's what happens: it is normal for every web browser, when you go to any web page, to automatically download all the image and text files on the web page to a temporary folder on the individual's computer. This makes browsing faster, and the web pages render quickly. The attacker encrypted and hid the malware in an image file so when the person goes to the page, they don't have to click on anything, mouse over anything, or agree to download anything. It happens automatically. This is often referred to as a drive-by download.

The more sophisticated malware doesn't create any files on the system, so there's nothing for your antivirus or antimalware program to detect; the malware runs in memory. Once it starts running, the system and your network are compromised. The attacker has successfully breached your organization. No one yet knows that the attackers have their foothold in your company. They start hiding all traces of their presence and remain hidden in plain sight. The attacker's next step is to steal network login credentials and start moving laterally to compromise other systems on the network that they can use to get in and out of your network in case that original system is off line or someone detects and deletes the compromise. Finally, the attacker starts mapping your network looking for your main systems and data servers, and most importantly, locating your crown jewels.

They now have the keys to the kingdom!

Can your CISO deploy technologies to prevent a successful breach using the attack vectors as described above? The answer is YES!

The Fix:

There are technologies to address these major holes, but you must provide your CISO the resources to implement these leading-edge technologies. We will discuss in a later chapter the specific technologies needed.

The above technique is how many large enterprises are successfully breached. But let's assume you are in the minority and have deployed cutting edge technology to prevent being breached in this manner. Can the attacker still gain entry? Yes, they can. In their reconnaissance phase of the mission, they learned of many of your 3rd party vendors and look to small to mid-size 3rd parties to attack and use them as a pivot point to gain entry into your company.

Medium Size Organizations

Since many large enterprises are well defended, sometimes referred to as hard targets, the attackers shift their attacks to softer targets – the medium size organizations. In PwC's 2015 survey on the Global State of Information Security[16], they found that breaches of mid-size companies increased by 64% from 2013 to 2014. That number continues to rise because medium size businesses are unable to, or choose not to, invest in sophisticated cyber security tools, technologies, and personnel, as the large enterprises do. Often they outsource their security to a Managed Security Services Provider (MSSP), but because they do not know what to ask for and/or they want to keep the costs as low as possible, the monitoring they receive is minimal and they do not get any immediate incident response in the event the MSSP discovers suspicious activity.

In mid-size businesses you will often not see a CISO position, and they often do not invest in dedicated cyber security teams. Again, they fall back on the myth that cyber security is an IT function and so have their IT personnel performing some security functions in addition to their

---

16. PwC Global State of Information Security Survey,
http://www.pwc.com/gx/en/issues/cyber-security/information-security-survey.html

normal IT responsibilities. There is a lack of funding, technologies, and time invested in properly securing the organization. Also you will see a lack of security awareness training and education. The security culture is non-existent.

What makes this lack of security even more incredible is that in today's world mid-sized organizations have very similar complex environments to the large enterprises, just at a smaller scale. They are interconnecting their offices across the country or internationally. They are using cloud-based systems for email, data storage, and other business services. Their employees are using mobile devices to work and connect back to the main company infrastructure. Vendors and partners are remotely accessing the company networks to perform services. If you are doing the same or similar type of business activities as large enterprises, then why wouldn't you implement the same type of cyber security services and activities? Why make it easy for the attackers to breach you?

The Attack:

Like with enterprise size organizations, attackers use the same approach as described earlier in sending spear phishing email to select individuals within the company. The major difference is that the attackers will not have to use a zero-day exploit to breach the organization. Zero-days are like gold, so they don't like to waste them if they don't have to. Fortunately for most attackers, when they go after the medium size business, the security profile is much lower and there are many vulnerabilities for the attacker to choose to exploit.

Depending on whether or not the mid-size business was the primary target or not, once inside, the attacker will search for and steal the company's intellectual property, trade secrets, sensitive business data, as well as any customer information, credit cards, health information, or anything else of value. The per capita cost of a breach is significantly higher for a mid-size organization than an enterprise. For example, an enterprise might be able to weather a $200 million cost for a breach, but a $10 million breach for a medium size company could put them out of business, particularly if their IP was lost as well.

The Fix:

What is the best approach for a mid-size company if they cannot afford to invest in a CISO and a comprehensive cyber security program? The first step is to identify the crown jewels of the company and exactly where they are located within the company.

Next, hire a cyber security consultant with Fortune 500 experience to conduct a strategic cyber security assessment to see exactly where the business is in terms of its security profile. The consultant will provide a strategic plan that outlines exactly what the company needs to do to raise its security profile. There might be low hanging fruit that the company can perform itself that pays big dividends in terms of security. If the company does have a cyber security team, then the plan will outline in a prioritized list what the team needs to do, what tools it might need, and whether or not additional headcount is needed. If the company plans to outsource security, then the consultant will help prepare a Request for Proposal (RFP) for outsourcing to a MSSP. The consultant also will help in evaluating the RFP responses, and assist in selecting a quality vendor. He/she also will help in preparing a comprehensive contract that will provide the best protection to the business. Finally, the consultant will assist the business in determining if it will purchase cyber insurance or not. We discuss the pros and cons of cyber insurance in a later chapter.

Small Businesses

Small businesses face an added threat of not only being a target to use as a pivot point to get into larger organizations, but they also face the risk of being a target of opportunity. According to Symantec, in 2014 sixty percent of all targeted attacks were directed against small to mid-sized businesses. Small target, big opportunity!

Small businesses often fall victim to the myth that because they are small no one would want to attack them. As we've discussed earlier, we know this is not true. Even large nation state attackers and organized crime groups go after small businesses because they are easy targets to breach. Once they breach a small business they can take control of all their systems without the business knowing it. From within the small company they can send email that contains malware to their larger partners, or they can take advantage of any VPN or remote access connections into a larger partner, and then use those connections to exploit the larger company.

The Attack:

Because small businesses often don't have good security awareness training programs, or even the tools to detect malware in email attachments, attackers more frequently use malware embedded in email attachments as a method of attack, as small business employees are more apt to open an attachment just to see what it is. This lack of awareness and security culture also places the company at risk of being a target of opportunity by any nefarious hacker.

Each and every day hackers run automated vulnerability scans against all Internet Protocol addresses. Security tools found in larger organizations normally block these types of scans. When the automated hacker tool finds a potentially vulnerable system it notifies the hacker who then attempts to breach the site. They might have no idea who or what the site is or its contents until after they breach it and get in. Once they are in, they then search out anything of value.

A major threat for many small businesses victimized as targets of opportunity is ransomware. When the hacker gets into the organization, it runs malware on key business servers and/or data storage locations. The malware encrypts these systems where only the attacker can unlock them. They send a ransom note to the company demanding large sums of money and instructions on how to pay. They usually put a deadline in which to receive payment. If payment is not received, the attacker can completely erase the systems. While larger organizations can tolerate the loss of servers, small businesses normally cannot, and their backups of the data are often not done regularly and effectively to rebuild new systems and restore their data if necessary. To make matters worse, even if they rebuilt their systems, if they didn't completely find and mitigate the attackers from their network, the attackers could potentially take down the new servers. How long can your small business survive with your main servers being held hostage, or your ecommerce web server(s) taken offline? What if the attacker decided to deface your web server(s) by telling all your customers you were hacked and they have all the customer data? Could you survive the loss of business let alone the legal costs of class action lawsuits?

The Fix:

So what can a small business do? There are many new security companies today who focus on providing managed security services for small size businesses. They are appropriately priced and provide a level of security that the small business could not normally perform on its own.

If this is still not an option for the small business owner, then you must hire at least one person dedicated to cyber security. There are several government and other organizations that provide free self-help guides for small businesses, including checklists of things to look for and how they can be fixed. I developed one of these while serving as the CISO for the Federal Communications Commission. It is still available today for download.[17] Also, look at organizations like US-CERT, the US Small Business Association, NIST, Get Cyber Safe (in Canada), or just Google it. The bottom line is you are a target and must do your due diligence in protecting your business, your data, and the data of your customers.

Visualizing the Threat

Now that we are clear on how organizations can be attacked, let's talk about the type of hackers present. The majority of attackers can be categorized into the following categories:

1. Nation States

2. Organized Crime

3. Terrorists or Extremists

4. Hackers and Hacktivists

5. Industrial Spies

6. Insiders

With a better understanding of who the attackers are, it should leave no doubt in the minds of any executive that every organization, regardless of

---

17. https://www.fcc.gov/general/cybersecurity-small-business

size or industry, is a target that can and will be breached. It is not a question of if your organization will be breached, but when.

One the most well-known military generals in history, Sun Tzu, said in his treatise The Art of War, which is the most famous and influential military strategy classic of all time, that "the only way to defeat your enemy is to know your enemy." This is as true today as it was 2,500 years ago when Sun Tzu was conquering nations in what is now eastern China. So let's take a closer look at each category of attackers to get a better understanding of who is attacking your networks.

Nation-States

These are countries that either are conducting attacks on other governments, countries, or businesses within those other countries, or provide the tacit approval, and often times resources, for hacker groups within their country to conduct cyber attacks against targets in other countries. There are many reasons why nation states conduct cyber espionage. Sometimes the purpose is military or defense related. The government wants to steal the secret information on new military technologies so that they can then develop technologies that can counter or defeat the new technologies of their adversaries. Related to that, but with an economic aspect, is that rather than spending millions of dollars and many years of research and development, they can steal the information, then manufacture the technology cheaper and faster than other countries.

In recent years we have seen examples of nation state attacks against US businesses for ideological or personal vengeance reasons. One such ideological or vengeance attack happened to Sony Pictures Entertainment..

In November 2014, North Korea attacked and successfully breached Sony Pictures Entertainment networks for making a comedy movie, *The Interview*, that depicted the assassination of North Korean leader Kim Jong Un. The malicious actors stole and publicly released nearly one hundred terabytes of Sony's sensitive data and information, including personal information of Sony executives and their families, salary information, and a few unreleased Sony movies. Following the theft of data, the attackers then ran malware that erased all the data on Sony's servers.

There is a very strong probability that the attack on Sony could have been either prevented or contained so quickly that any damage or loss of data would have been minimal. The Board of Directors and the C-Suite executives should have made cyber security a high priority for the organization and implemented leading-edge technologies to protect the business from these kinds of attacks.

What makes nation state attackers the most serious threat in the world? Their government backs them so they have unlimited financial resources. They have no shortage of funds or personnel. They buy or otherwise acquire every security technology and operating system available and then spend extensive amounts of time to find vulnerabilities in these systems. They then develop malware to exploit these vulnerabilities. When attacking an organization, during their reconnaissance phase, they learn about their target's network and the tools they use. They then build a network similar to the target and run their attacks in their lab before using it on the actual target. This helps them not only more easily breach the organization, but also learn how to stay under the radar and not be detected.

In some nation states, they use their military in addition to civilian and contract employees. They have specific, fairly large military units that are very well trained, organized, and highly sophisticated. These military units operate 24x7 and conduct their cyber attacks just like any other military operation. They are extremely effective and successful.

Organized Crime

On December 13, 2013, Target executives get a call from the US Department of Justice. The FBI urgently wants to talk to them. This is not good news! The CIO knows that when the FBI calls and the CIO has to be in the meeting, it usually means one thing – a breach. And that is exactly what it meant in this case. Target had been breached and customer credit cards were being sold on the black market. Timing couldn't be worse, as it's right in the middle of the biggest sales time of the year – the Christmas shopping season.

The questions are coming by the dozens: How could this happen? We have security tools. We have leading-edge technology. We passed our last PCI compliance audit. Who did it? How did they get in? What did they steal? How much did they steal? How long have they been in? Who do we call to fix this? To whom and when do we report this –SEC, FTC, merchant banks, customers, our Board?

All too often we have seen attackers breach an organization many months, sometimes years, before they are discovered. In 2014, the average time an attacker was on a network before discovery was seven months. If that was the case with Target, how many tens of millions of additional credit card numbers could these criminals have stolen? Reportedly, forensics later discovered the attackers breached Target on November 27, 2013. That's only 16 days. How bad could it be?

Panic. Anger. Frustration. Fear. A multitude of emotions hitting all at the same time. OK, quickly get our CISO in here to fix this. Oh wait, we don't have a CISO! We're a Fortune 100 company with over $75B in revenue and we don't have a CISO?

We know the rest of the story was not good. In the short period of time that the criminals were on Target's networks, they were able to steal 40 million Target credit card numbers and the private data of an additional 70 million customers. Both the CEO and CIO resigned.

These criminals are motivated by financial gain. Since 2008, organized crime has significantly increased their cyber operations, as high rewards and low risk make it an extremely attractive global and very profitable business. Many of the organized crime groups today take advantage of countries that have weak jurisdiction and enforcement of cyber-crimes. Many of these countries do not have either the necessary laws or the cyber security technologies to detect and prosecute cyber-criminals. Since this industry is so profitable for the criminals, they are able to always purchase the latest and best malware and hacking tools available on the Internet.

While some organized crime groups have teams of hackers, they really do not have to have all that many to be effective. In today's world, we see a lot of organized crime groups that rent or buy attack tools and technologies on the Internet and the Dark Web. Attackers can rent botnets (a group of thousands or tens of thousands of compromised computers that can be used for attacks) by the week, month, or year. Similarly, they can buy the most sophisticated malware available that comes with instructions, videos, and in some cases technical support. These groups use very sophisticated hacking tools and malware, and some are on par with nation state attackers.

Some organized crime groups focus on attacking financial services organizations, while others attack any business in which they think that they can squeeze a ransom from the company. What they ransom is the company's own data. They will hack into the organization and use very sophisticated malware called "root kits" that allow the attacker to remain hidden and undetected from traditional antimalware systems. They then operate freely on the network and search for sensitive company information, intellectual property, trade secrets, financial data, and anything else of value. Once stolen, they contact the company for a ransom threatening to either release the information publicly, or to sell the information to their competitors.

In February 2016, the Hollywood Presbyterian Medical Center in California was the victim of a ransomware attack.[18] The attackers demanded a $3.6 million ransom to be in Bitcoin, a type of digital currency created and held electronically. No one controls it, thus making it extremely hard to track. At the time of writing, the hospital had not yet paid the ransom and was working with the FBI and the LAPD; however, the hospital computers, and access to patient data, radiology systems, pharmacy and much more were down for over a week. Staff was forced to record all information manually and to upload later if and when the criminals released the systems. If they fail to pay, or they fail to figure out how to eliminate the ransomware and unencrypt the systems and data, the criminals may destroy everything.

Organized criminals also target many organizations that have point of sale (POS) systems that process credit card transactions for their customers. They will breach the company, or possibly one of the supply chain vendors, to gain access to the company's network. Once inside the network they

---

18. Ransomware takes Hollywood hospital offline, $3.6M demanded by attackers.
   http://www.csoonline.com/article/3033160/security/ransomware-takes-hollywood-hospital-offline-36m-demanded-by-attackers.html

look for the transactional databases that contain all the transactions from the POS systems. They also search for the actual networks where the POS systems reside and launch malware directly at the POS systems to capture customer data in real time. The attackers will then create a hidden file share where they collect all this information. Then they encrypt it and break it up into smaller files and export the data to their malicious servers.

Most of the large security software firms estimate that the global cost of cyber-crime, including mitigation, lost business, and even ransom payments, is in excess of US $100 billion per year.

Terrorist or Extremists

This group includes nation states, terrorist organizations, and extremist organizations. These groups typically would target critical infrastructure protection, government organizations, the transportation industry, and the financial services industry. However, like with nation state attackers described above, these groups might target supply chain vendors to use as a pivot point and potential avenue to get into their primary target.

The distinction between nation state attackers and the groups here is that in the earlier group it is the nation state itself conducting the attacks, meaning whether it be military personnel or civilian, they work directly for the nation state. In this group, it is more of a terrorist-like organization that is condoned by the nation state, or is purposely ignored. These groups may or may not receive funding and resources from the nation state.

A terrorist group such as ISIS (Islamic State of Iraq and Syria) is an example of a group that has significantly improved their cyber-attack and exploitation capabilities as of late. Attacks of this type might be for financial gain to support their operations, or they could be as a diversion before a physical attack.

Hackers and Hacktivists

These groups typically have some kind of geo-political or social agenda and will hack into organizations in order to embarrass them by finding and publishing sensitive and/or personal information about the company, its business dealings, or its senior executives. The main concern with these types of groups is the brand or reputation damage that they can cause. They tend to range in experience from beginner to very advanced. The beginners are out to make a name for themselves and establish their "street credentials." Often they are referred to as script kiddies, as they download hacking tools from the Internet and run preprogrammed attack scripts to try and breach an organization.

The more advanced groups, for example, Anonymous, Lulzsec, Antisec, are quite sophisticated and capable. They have successfully breached hundreds, if not thousands, of organizations. How good are they?

Well, on Feb 5, 2011, the CEO of computer security firm HBGary Federal, Aaron Barr, announced that his company had successfully infiltrated Anonymous. HBGary Federal provided cyber services and tools to the US Government and other large companies. They also provided "offensive" tools. In other words, they would hack other businesses and individuals doing whatever their client wanted. The day after Mr. Barr's announcement, Anonymous started an attack on HBGary Federal. They took down the company's website and replaced the home page with a letter from Anonymous that read in part: "You brought this upon yourself. You've tried to bite at the Anonymous hand, and now the Anonymous hand is bitch-slapping you in the face." They continued the attack and breached the HBGary networks. They took, and later made public, 68,000 private and sensitive emails, many of which indicated that HBGary was working on behalf of Bank of America and several other companies trying to take down or prevent release of information on WikiLeaks. Other emails appear to show that the US Chamber of Commerce hired HBGary to spy on and discredit unions and other liberal groups[19]. Anonymous also took down HBGary Federal's phone systems and erased files. They didn't stop there. They posted personal information about the CEO such as his home address and social security number.[20]

This is very typical of how these groups operate. For any ideological reason they have, they will hack into a company, and expose sensitive business

19. https://en.wikipedia.org/wiki/HBGary
20. https://en.wikipedia.org/wiki/Timeline_of_events_associated_with_Anonymous

and personal information about the company and its executives. They also successfully breached the website of the US Central Intelligence Agency and numerous other governments around the world. They have attacked US businesses such as Monsanto, Sony, Bay Area Rapid Transit, and others for their own political agenda and/or reasons.

Industrial Spies

This group of attackers targets companies for the theft of their Intellectual Property (IP) for their own economic gain or simply to sell this information to a competitor of the victim company. Industrial espionage is the biggest economic threat to businesses across the US and the rest of the world. Loss of IP can result in losing competitive advantage, a significant loss in market share, and loss of revenue and profitability.

Industrial espionage is an age-old concern for business owners, but in today's cyber connected world it makes it much easier for industrial spies to break into a company and steal its trade secrets. Also, by conducting the espionage through cyber methods, attribution of who actually stole the information is much more difficult. It takes the term "competitive intelligence" to a new level. Not only can these spies steal intellectual property and trade secrets, but they can also steal and publish sensitive, potentially embarrassing information, and either blackmail the company or discredit it by publicly "leaking" the information.

In 2009, Starwood Hotels accused Hilton Hotels of stealing confidential information on Starwood's luxury hotel brand "W," which was introduced in 1998 and has been very successful. Hilton was interested in starting its own luxury brand they were going to call Denizon. Starwood claimed Hilton stole over 10,000 documents and were using this confidential information to create their luxury brand. After an extended investigation and litigation, Hilton paid Starwood a $75 million settlement and accepted a court order ban on developing the Denizon brand of luxury hotels or any others for at least two years.[21]

---

21. Hilton Paid Starwood $75 Million in Espionage Settlement
    https://en.wikipedia.org/wiki/Timeline_of_events_associated_with_Anonymous

Insiders

This group is one of the hardest groups to detect and can be one of the most damaging. Insiders can be industrial spies who applied for a job within the company for the sole purpose of stealing IP. Insiders are also disgruntled employees who might have been passed over for promotion or a new position, or just don't like their supervisor, or many other reasons. Their activities range from uploading or installing malware on the corporate network, to giving a malicious attacker access credentials so an external attacker can gain internal access, or they might want to steal IP for their own personal gain whether to sell it to the highest bidder or use it to gain a better position in a competitor company. There are many ways the insider can steal this information. They can load terabytes of data on a thumb drive, upload data to a cloud based storage system such as Dropbox, they can email the data, or even print it out and carry out the printed information in their pockets.

Insiders account for approximately 43% of all data breaches; half are intentional and half are unintentional. In a recent Intel Security report,[22] in 68% of incidents studied, the data exfiltrated from the network was serious enough to require public disclosure or have a negative financial impact on the company.

So with that said, the million-dollar (or billion dollar) question remains: Am I a target?

With a better understanding of who the attackers are, it should leave no doubt in the minds of any executive that every organization, regardless of size or industry, is a target that can and will be breached. As we have seen with so many other breaches, the organizations had security in place and thought they were secure and properly monitoring; yet, when they were notified by external agencies or discovered a malicious actor on their network, they found that the attacker had been on their networks for many, many months.

---

22. Grand Theft Data, http://www.mcafee.com/us/resources/reports/rp-data-exfiltration.pdf

Fact or Fiction?

Now that you understand the threats and know who the attackers are, it's time to separate the fact from the fiction surrounding cyber security. Let's take a look at the five biggest myths in cyber security. Clarity in these areas will help you to better evaluate and analyze where your focus needs to be with regards to cyber security within your organization.

MYTH #1: We've never been breached, so our security must be good.

Nothing could be farther from the truth. Just because you've never had a heart attack doesn't mean that you will never have one. You can't take the approach that you don't need to closely and properly manage your health. Similarly, there are many things you must do to ensure your cyber security health. You must task your cyber doctor, your CISO, to build a comprehensive cyber security program. However, you must provide your CISO with the necessary resources to do so. Providing only lip service that cyber security is important is a recipe for disaster. With the proper resources, and bringing in third party consultants, your CISO can dive deep into your systems and networks to determine exactly what your security posture is and what is needed to prevent a major breach.

MYTH #2: We've invested millions in cyber security, so we will not be breached.

Many companies today think that by having firewalls, intrusion detection/ prevention systems, and antivirus tools they will be protected. This is a complete myth. These security technologies alone are far from capable of stopping a determined attacker. In fact, most companies go so far as to help the attackers. They don't just leave the back door open; they leave the front door wide open with no guard and a big welcome sign flashing over it. There are Fortune 100 companies who have eight and nine-figure annual cyber security budgets, yet still have been breached. This isn't to say that you shouldn't make significant investments into your cyber security. Following JPMorgan Chase's breach in 2014, CEO Jamie Dimon said that over the next five years they will probably double their current $250 million annual budget for cyber security. He went on to say,

"It's about firewall protection, it's about internal protection, it's about vendor protection, it's about everything that hooks up into you. There will be a lot of battles. Unfortunately, some will be lost."[23]

The keys here are to first know exactly what your crown jewels are and where they are located, so that your CISO can properly secure them, so that when you are breached, the attacker cannot get to them. Secondly, you must have an extremely good and well-practiced incident response program. Your incident responders must be able to react to a security incident within minutes of detection, not hours, days, or weeks. The faster you can react and contain the breach, the less damage and data loss that will occur.

MYTH #3: We're a small company, so we won't be attacked.

This is a very common misconception. SMB leaders often think that they are a small business, or are in an industry that wouldn't be of interest to an attacker. It should go without saying that all large enterprises and most medium-sized organizations are being attacked every day; however, all other businesses also are subject to attack.

Fazio Mechanical Services is a small HVAC company based in Pittsburg, PA. Their CEO Ross Fazio believed that they were in full compliance with industry practices for IT system and security measures. He probably wasn't too concerned about being attacked or breached by a nation state or organized crime, as they are a relatively small company that just provides heating, air conditioning, and refrigeration services to supermarket chains and other companies. Who would want to breach them? Well, someone did. The attacker sent spear phishing email to several Fazio employees who opened the email resulting in the compromise of the company. Two months later, using credentials stolen from Fazio, the attackers breached Target.

This was not an isolated event of a small company, or a company in a non-descript industry being attacked and used as a pivot point to attack a larger, better protected company. This is a regular occurrence.

---

23. Dimon Sees Cyber-Security Spending Doubling After Hack,
    http://www.bloomberg.com/news/articles/2014-10-10/dimon-sees-jpmorgan-doubling-250-million-cyber-security-budget

MYTH #4: We're 100% compliant, so we must be secure.

Please take note – compliance does NOT equate to security! Too often we see in organizations that their cyber security focus is directed towards compliance. While compliance is important to meet regulatory requirements, it is only a small subset of what is required in a comprehensive cyber security program. Regulatory controls are minimum standards of security controls that must be applied. It often takes quite some time for regulators to make changes to security controls; consequently, they can't keep up with the ever-changing vulnerabilities and attack vectors. Further, the prescribed security controls do not define specific security technologies for advanced threat detection capabilities.

In one of my early CISO assignments, the position was created, in part, because my organization had miserably failed a compliance inspection. They knew they needed to find a solution. Over the course of the first year, I made sure we were 100% compliant and had a solid compliance program in place. When the auditors came back the following year, we passed with flying colors and the auditors lauded us and said we had a model program that others should emulate. My senior executives were extremely happy, patting me on the back, and praising my efforts. All the while I was thinking in my head that our cyber security program, at best, was a C+! But at least we started by implementing a game plan to protect crucial data and information.

MYTH #5: Cyber Security is an IT Function.

As you probably have figured out by now, this is my all-time favorite myth. It is one on which I am constantly having to educate others. In earlier chapters, we discussed the need to separate the governance and oversight portion (cyber security) from the hands on implementers (IT), and also the requirement to allocate a separate budget for the cyber security department.

As we have seen from the many breaches of recent years, the amount of brand and reputation damage, loss of shareholder value, litigation from class action lawsuits, and all the other significant costs associated with a breach, have elevated cyber security to the attention of the board and out of IT. Cyber security is, or should be, a key component of your organization's strategic risk management framework. The same level of due diligence that is performed for other business risk analysis must be done for cyber security as well.

There must be a divergence of cyber security from IT and a convergence with your business operations. The empirical data shows that the CISO reporting to the CEO or the Board of Directors, instead of the CIO, significantly reduces downtime and financial losses resulting from cyber security incidents. Cyber security supports all aspects of the business. The CISO works closely with all the business leaders to assist them in being more productive and innovative in a secure manner.

Size Really Does Matter

It doesn't matter how big or how small you are – cyber security is a conversation all organizations should have. This chapter has provided you with a better understanding of the risk to your specific type of business, along with the different threats to each of these categories. We discussed the anatomy of an attack and how difficult it is for seasoned cyber security professionals to detect and defend against these types of attacks without the proper resources, people, processes, and technologies. Taking a page from Sun Tzu's philosophy of knowing your enemy in order to defeat him, we took a close look at the different categories of attackers and their motivations. Finally, we closed with most common myths surrounding cyber security.

Armed with this information, you are now much better prepared to start framing your cyber security program and your plan of attack. In the next chapter, we will examine the impacts of a cyber security breach. If this chapter didn't get your attention on why cyber security is so important, the next chapter definitely will.

Chapter 4:

Damage Done: *Understanding the Impact of a Breach*

Cyber security is no longer a convenience for any business. It is now an absolute necessity. To this point, you have likely seen the substantial and sometimes irreversible damage a breach can cause. If you aren't inspired by now to take a second look at the infrastructure within your business, you are just a sitting duck surrounded by experienced predators. In short, your days are numbered. Before we go into the details of how to create a rock solid cyber security program, let's dive a little deeper into the impact that a breach can have on your organization.

How Deep Does it Go?

It is a lack of understanding on the part of Boards and C-Suites that causes them to improperly invest in cyber security. They really just don't get it. That is, until they are victimized by a squatter looking for an unsuspecting target. As demonstrated in the major breaches recently seen, the impact of these breaches extends far beyond the direct cost of incident response – containing, mitigating, and recovery operations. Brand and reputation damage will result in a loss of current and future customers, revenue, or likely both. Other ancillary effects include negative impact to shareholder value and share price, loss of intellectual property, proprietary data, and the dissemination of sensitive business information that erodes competitive advantage, class action lawsuits, and more.

Let's look at a few of these and see how they can impact your organization.

Brand and Reputation Damage

While brand is considered an intangible asset, it is often one of the most valuable to an organization. It also is the area hardest to estimate regarding the financial impact it can have on your business. There have been numerous studies that all agree on one thing – subsequent to a major cyber security breach there will be damage to the brand and reputation of the company that will reduce its future revenue. Here are a few of the results:

- The Lares Institute[24] study shows that 40% of consumers make their buying decisions based on privacy. If the consumer feels the business is poor at protecting their personal information, they will go elsewhere.

Cyber security is no longer a convenience for any business. It is now an absolute necessity. To this point, you have likely seen the substantial and sometimes irreversible damage a breach can cause. If you aren't inspired by now to take a second look at the infrastructure within your business, you are just a sitting duck surrounded by experienced predators. In short, your days are numbered. Before we go into the details of how to create a rock solid cyber security program, let's dive a little deeper into the impact that a breach can have on your organization.

How Deep Does it Go?

It is a lack of understanding on the part of Boards and C-Suites that causes them to improperly invest in cyber security. They really just don't get it. That is, until they are victimized by a squatter looking for an unsuspecting target. As demonstrated in the major breaches recently seen, the impact of these breaches extends far beyond the direct cost of incident response – containing, mitigating, and recovery operations. Brand and reputation damage will result in a loss of current and future customers, revenue, or likely both. Other ancillary effects include negative impact to shareholder value and share price, loss of intellectual property, proprietary data, and the dissemination of sensitive business information that erodes competitive advantage, class action lawsuits, and more.

Let's look at a few of these and see how they can impact your organization.

Brand and Reputation Damage

While brand is considered an intangible asset, it is often one of the most valuable to an organization. It also is the area hardest to estimate regarding the financial impact it can have on your business. There have been numerous studies that all agree on one thing – subsequent to a major cyber security breach there will be damage to the brand and reputation of the company that will reduce its future revenue. Here are a few of the results:

- The Lares Institute[24] study shows that 40% of consumers make their buying decisions based on privacy. If the consumer feels the business is poor at protecting their personal information, they will go elsewhere.
- In a Raytheon study[25] on the online behavior of millennials, 60% were a victim of a cyber event, of which 70% changed their online behavior and 27% abandoned purchases because of concerns around privacy and their personal data.
- Edelman's 2015 The Trust Barometer[26] showed that 80% of consumers place privacy of their personal data as their top priority when evaluating brands they trust.
- In a HyTrust survey,[27] 52% of consumers said that they would take their business elsewhere if a company they were doing business with was breached.

The numbers don't lie. It is very difficult to determine the associated cost of losing existing customers or failing to gain new customers because of a consumer perception of a lack of security within your organization. Could your business afford to lose 50% of your existing customers? Can you afford to lose in an instant the consumer trust in your brand and reputation you have worked for so many years to build? To lose your competitive advantage? Restoration of your brand could easily take a year or longer.

Intellectual Property

We described earlier how former Fortune 500 industry leader Nortel Networks was a victim of cyber espionage and lost their intellectual

---

24. The Business Case for Privacy, http://www.laresinstitute.com/archives/4571
25. Preparing Millennials to Lead in Cyberspace, www.staysafeonline.org/download/datasets/10610/Raytheon survey 2014.pdf
26. Edelman's 2015 The Trust Barometer
    http://www.edelman.com/insights/intellectual-property/2015-edelman-trust-barometer/
27. Consumers Increasingly Hold Companies Responsible for Loss of Confidential Information,
    http://www.hytrust.com/sites/default/files/HyTrust_consumer_poll_results_with_charts2.pdf

property, which forced them into bankruptcy, essentially ending their business operations. It is not just the loss of IP that can negatively impact the business in these cases, but also the loss of any sensitive business information. It can be research & development, merger & acquisition, proprietary information, patented data, or anything else that gives your company a competitive advantage in the marketplace.

One wouldn't immediately think that white paint would be the target of a high priority cyber espionage mission for one of the largest countries in the world, yet it was, as we will see below. It requires the chemical titanium dioxide, also known as titanium white, to make quality white paint. This chemical also is used in making paper, plastics, cosmetics, and other consumer goods.

It's a $17B global industry of which DuPont controlled 20%. According to the FBI report,[28] DuPont refused to sell its proprietary manufacturing process to China. The Chinese turned around, making the development and production of titanium white a scientific and economic priority, and launched a plan to steal the information from DuPont. They recruited and hired DuPont employees of Chinese descent, appealing to their Chinese ethnicity, and convinced them to work for the good of the PRC. The Chinese paid at least one of the individuals millions and contracted with him to build and run a factory in China. Years later, he and his accomplices were arrested and convicted, but the damage was done. China has gained a 22% share of the market space, and between 2012 and 2014 dropped the price of their titanium dioxide, now being manufactured based on the DuPont processes, over $1,000 a ton, which significantly lowered DuPont's market share, revenue, and profits on this product.

Theft of IP is nothing new. It has been around for as long as there have been businesses and disreputable people and/or companies trying to steal this sensitive information to gain a competitive market advantage.

US businesses alone annually lose billions of dollars in IP theft. Putting an exact dollar figure on the amount is difficult for a number of reasons.

---

28. The IP Commission Report, http://www.ipcommission.org/report/ip_commission_report_052213.pdf

First, in many cases, bringing a new product or process to market could provide only a year of market advantage before competitors legitimately develop similar products or processes. However, in some cases, like with the DuPont product mentioned above, the advantage could last several years. There are also many companies who do not know that they have been, or are, victims of IP theft. That loss might still be occurring, as they have not invested in a cyber security program that could detect and stop that loss. Still, there are other companies that choose not to even report the losses.

As leaders of your organization, you should foresee this threat as you grow your business, particularly if you expand into international markets. As the size of your networks increases with each new location that you open or acquire, the threat of data loss increases. You should ask yourself and your CISO the following questions:

- Are you protecting these networks in the same manner that you are your corporate HQ?
- How are you managing the oversight of your 3rd party vendors and partners in international locations?
- Are your foreign national employees and vendors properly vetted, and do they have access to sensitive business information?
- What are the data security laws in the countries you are operating in?

The answers to these questions will provide you with more detailed and helpful information to fully understand if an additional investment for the new location or acquisition is required. And if so, they will help you to better assess the valuation knowing the additional costs that will be required to properly secure your data there.

Class Action Lawsuits

Over the past few years, the number of class action lawsuits has substantially increased, and we see them initiated as soon as a couple of days after the public announcement of the breach. Some are initiated by individuals and some are initiated by financial institutions. Target, Wyndham Worldwide, TJX Companies, Heartland Payment Systems, Home Depot, Anthem, and others have all had class action lawsuits filed against them. In fact, in the above cases the plaintiffs' legal team has filed shareholder derivative litigation against the directors.

There were 33 separate class action lawsuits filed with Target. In April 2014, a US Multidistrict Judicial Panel consolidated them into a single lawsuit.[29] On November 17, 2015, a federal judge in Minnesota approved the final judgment for $10M, with up to $10,000 to individual customers who were victims of identity theft or suffered losses on their credit cards because of the breach. This was in addition to a $67 million settlement with Visa, agreeing to compensate thousands of financial institutions for the costs they suffered as a result of the breach. It has already cost Target in excess of $200 million in breach related costs, of which $21 million was for legal and other professional services.

At the time of writing (2016), Home Depot has 44 civil actions pending against it due to the data breach, and on September 2, 2015 a derivative lawsuit was filed against twelve directors and officers alleging they breached "their fiduciary duties of loyalty, good faith, and due care by knowingly and in conscious disregard of their duties failing to ensure that Home Depot took reasonable measures to protect its customers' personal and financial information."[30]

What we see in the Home Depot filing is typical in these cases where the plaintiffs' lawyers will charge that the directors and officers:

- Failed to implement a comprehensive cyber security program
- Failed to protect consumer and employee personal or financial information
- Failed to do their due diligence and oversight by ignoring cyber security risks

You don't have to be breached by a nation state or organized crime to have a class action lawsuit filed against you for a data loss. Look at the example

---

29. $10M Target Data Breach Settlement Obtains Final Approval,
   http://topclassactions.com/lawsuit-settlements/lawsuit-news/237688-target-10m-setfinal-approval/
30. Data Breach-Related Derivative Lawsuit Filed against Home Depot Directors and Officers,
   http://www.dandodiary.com/2015/09/articles/cyber-liability/data-breach-related-derivative-lawsuit-filed-against-home-depot-directors-and-officers/

of AvMed Health Plans. They provide health plans to individuals and businesses in Florida. In December 2009, they had two laptops stolen, which contained the personal data of over 1 million customers.

Subsequently, a class action lawsuit was filed and in 2014 a Florida federal judge awarded a $3.1M settlement[31] stating that AvMed was negligent in not protecting the data of its customers. What's interesting about this case is that the judge allowed payments to all customers whose data was lost including those that did not suffer any financial loss or identity theft. How could AvMed have avoided brand and reputation damage, 4-5 years of litigation, and a $3M settlement? Simply by having and implementing a cyber security policy that states all mobile devices, particularly laptops, will have full disk encryption.

If you are thinking that you, as a board member, are protected from liability by an exculpation clause in your organization's corporate charter, well that is changing as well. Board members are being held personally liable. In fact, at least one state, Delaware, prohibits exculpation for breaches of the duty of good faith, or as we explain in more detail later in the Caremark case, oversight liability.

Even if you win the class action lawsuit and prove you did your due diligence, the legal fees alone can cost millions and drag on for years.

Fines

In addition to the class action lawsuits, federal government agencies, such as the Federal Trade Commission (FTC), Federal Communications Commission (FCC), Department of Health and Human Services (HHS), and the Securities and Exchange Commission (SEC), may conduct investigations that result in multi-million dollar fines and penalties. In some cases, they have directed that the organizations implement an effective cyber security and privacy program that is audited annually by an external third party.

---

31. $3M Data Breach Settlement Approved for AvMed Customers Unaffected by Identity Theft, http://www.winston.com/en/privacy-law-corner/3m-data-breach-settlement-approved-for-avmed-customers. htmlhttp://www.hytrust.com/sites/default/files/HyTrust_consumer_poll_results_with_charts2.pdf

In July 2015, LifeLock, a company that provides identity theft protection services to its customers, was charged by the FTC for violating the terms of a 2010 settlement with the FTC and with 35 state attorneys by continuing to make deceptive claims about its identity theft services as well as failing to protect the data of its customers.[32] The FTC levied fines up to $16,000 per consumer, per violation. The total in fines that LifeLock is subject to pay could amount to $116M. Following the announcement by the FTC on July 21, 2015, LifeLock's stock plummeted 50%.

In April 2015, the FCC assessed a $25M fine against AT&T for a data breach[33] that involved the disclosure of the personal information, including social security numbers, of 280,000 customers. "As the nation's expert agency on communications networks, the Commission cannot, and will not, stand idly by when a carrier's lax data security practices expose the personal information of hundreds of thousands of the most vulnerable Americans to identity theft and fraud," said FCC Chairman Tom Wheeler. "As today's action demonstrates, the Commission will exercise its full authority against companies that fail to safeguard the personal information of their customers."

In another case of failing to properly encrypt consumer data, the Financial Industry Regulatory Authority (FINRA) fined the financial services firm Stern Agee & Leach Inc. $225,000 for loss of an unencrypted laptop that contained confidential financial and personal information on over 350,000 customers.[34]

It seems that it would be a wise business investment to implement a comprehensive, effective cyber security program right away and avoid the embarrassment, reputation damage, and associated legal costs. One way or the other, you will eventually have to invest in cyber security. Doing it sooner rather than later is much more cost effective.

---

32. LifeLock Tentatively Settles with FTC, www.databreachtoday.com/lifelock-tentatively-settles-ftc-a-8641
33. AT&T To Pay $25M To Settle Investigation Into Three Data Breaches,
    https://www.fcc.gov/document/att-pay-25m-settle-investigation-three-data-breaches-0
34. FINRA Fines Financial Firm for Failing to Encrypt Customer Data on Lost Laptop, http://www.swlaw.com/blog/data-security/2015/06/19/finra-fines-financial-firm-for-failing-to-encrypt-customer-data-on-lost-laptop/

Damage Done

There are several examples of organizations that have gone out of business because of the impact caused by a cyber breach and loss of IP. One of the best known is that of Nortel Networks. Once a Fortune 500 company and North America's largest manufacturer of telephony equipment, they were breached by an Advanced Persistent Threat who remained hidden on their network for several years and stole their most sensitive data. Executive management failed to listen to the heeds of their CISO or provide the needed cyber security resources, and in 2009 Norton filed for bankruptcy. They are no longer in business.

It's not just the enterprise giants who are targets of cyber-crime. 60% of all attacks are aimed at small to medium sized businesses (SMB). If they are not attacked specifically for the information they possess, they could be used as a pivot point to gain entry into a larger enterprise. In either case, the end result is the same – the business is breached and it will suffer the costs of the damage done. While a Fortune 500 company might be able to withstand the loss of IP, the brand and reputation damage, and the many millions of dollars in breach related costs, a SMB might not be so lucky. The per capita cost of a breach is four times as much as a large enterprise. Research by security company Symantec shows that 60% of small businesses go out of business within six months of a cyber security breach.[35]

In some cases, it doesn't even take six months to force a company out of business. DigiNotar was a Dutch security company. Their main product was digital certificates; in fact, they were a Certificate Authority. They issued the certificates to businesses, websites, and individuals to use to validate encrypted sessions on the Internet. For example, when you go to your online banking website, or you make a purchase online, the session is encrypted using digital certificates from a Certificate Authority. DigiNotar was hacked in January 2011. They didn't discover the breach until June. In the interim, the attackers stole the certificates and manipulated them so that they could spy on anyone who was using these

---

35. SMB Data Breach Fallout, https://aerissecure.com/blog/smb-data-breach-fallout/

certificates. The Dutch government renounced their trust in the company shortly after the breach announcement. Also, the makers of web browsers blacklisted the DigiNotar certificates. In September they filed bankruptcy and went out of business.

A few observations from this breach investigation are useful for us. The investigators found that their firewalls and internal network devices were not properly configured nor were they audited. While there was quite a bit of network segmentation, they didn't apply proper access controls, so the attackers were able to easily move laterally around the network. DigiNotar's crown jewels were not properly segregated or protected. Monitoring of the network was ineffective at best. All of these areas would be properly taken care of with a comprehensive cyber security program.

Another company forced into bankruptcy due to a cyber security breach was Altegrity, Inc. Altegrity was a US government contractor that provided security services including data recovery and employment screening. The department within Altegrity that performed background investigations and employment screening was named US Investigations Service (USIS). In 2013, Altegrity was breached and over 25,000 records of personnel in the Department of Homeland Security, US Immigrations and Customs Enforcement, and others, including some undercover investigators, were stolen. Despite Altegrity's efforts to identify, self-report, and remediate the breach, the government lost confidence in their ability to properly protect this sensitive information and terminated two substantial contracts that accounted for 22% of Altegrity's revenue. Altegrity filed bankruptcy once they lost those contracts.

Set aside your moral views as we take a look at another interesting case that might force a company into bankruptcy, and possibly even put a big damper on a section of a niche industry.

Ashley Madison, and its Toronto-based parent company Avid Life Media, were the targets of a Hacktivist cyber attack. As we described in an earlier chapter, Hacktivists will attack businesses for any reason at all. It could be political or religious motivations or, as in this case, moral reasons. The group claiming responsibility for the attack is called Impact Team. They said they wanted to destroy Avid Life Media. They hacked into the Ashley Madison website, an adultery website where customers can find someone to cheat on their spouse with, and stole the database of 32 million past and current users.

The attackers, in the style of many hacktivists, gave the target an option to either take down the website permanently or face public release of the entire database. Avid Life Media refused to comply and the hacktivists published the database. Avid Life Media now faces a myriad of expensive class action and other lawsuits. Some of the interesting points here are that Ashley Madison had customers from all over the world. While a majority of the customers are based in the US, Avid Life Media could have to fight the same case in multiple countries around the world, as the privacy laws of many countries are much stricter than the US laws. And in this particular case, every exposed customer has had their reputation damaged (they were looking to cheat on their spouse), whereas in other data loss cases, the customers often have to prove that they have been the victims of identity theft or their credit cards have been fraudulently used. The final settlement, not including their legal fees, could easily run into hundreds of millions. Considering that they only grossed $115M in pre-tax revenue in 2014, this could result in the business filing bankruptcy and going under. It will be interesting to see if Avid Life Media does go bankrupt, and if so, if another company would be brave enough to take their place and risk being breached even if they had better security. Would consumers take a chance on using an adultery web site knowing their data could be exposed at any time?

The lessons learned in each of these examples are that, regardless of size, all organizations need to have an in-depth, well-practiced incident response program. Quick containment of a breach limits damage and significantly reduces costs. Additionally, doing your due diligence with a comprehensive, documented program will normally prevent a considerable loss of customer confidence.

Can You Be Held Liable for a Breach?

The bottom line is you can be held both professionally and personally liable for a breach. Between April 2008 and January 2010, Wyndham

Worldwide Corporation suffered from multiple cyber security breaches in which the attackers stole credit card data and Personally Identifiable Information (PII) from more than 619,000 customers, which later led to fraudulent charges estimated to be over $10.6 million.

The US government's Federal Trade Commission (FTC) believes that its charter is to protect consumers from unfair and deceptive trade practices, and took legal action against Wyndham for failing to provide adequate security for its data systems. Wyndham moved to dismiss by saying the FTC does not have the authority to pursue legal action against US businesses and the FTC had established no data security standards for which they were in violation.

Judge Esther Salas of the US District Court for the District of New Jersey disagreed with Wyndham. Wyndham appealed to the US Third Circuit Court of Appeals. The Third Circuit Court on August 24, 2015 upheld the ruling of the District Court. At the time of publication of this book (2016), the fines and penalties against Wyndham have not yet been determined; however, the key takeaway in this case is that there is now established case law authorizing the US Government to take legal actions and impose fines and penalties against US businesses for failing to employ reasonable cyber security measures in protecting against the loss of data of their customers and employees.

There is US case law in re Caremark International Derivative Litigation, Delaware Court of Chancery, that holds directors personally liable for duty of care (oversight) of their organizations. Now known as oversight liability, the Caremark case was based on the presumption that the directors "allowed a situation to develop and continue," which caused the corporation to suffer a loss and "that in doing so they violated a duty to be active monitors of corporate performance."[36]

If you are the CEO or the CIO, there is a good chance that you could be held personally liable. Think about that for a second. You could lose your house, your cars, and your retirement because of a cyber-breach under your

---

36. Caremark, 698 A.2d at 967

watchful eye. At the least, there's a very strong probability that you will lose your job, or be asked to resign, following a major cyber security breach, as was the case with the Target CEO Gregg Steinhafel, a 35-year employee of the company, and Target CIO, Beth Jacobs. Similarly, the co-chairman of Sony Pictures, Amy Pascal, and the Director of the US Office of Personnel Management, Katherine Archuleta, were asked to resign subsequent to breaches in their organizations. A new trend has started where senior executives, rather than the IT security persons, are being held responsible for the protection and security of the data within their organizations.

We have been focusing on those issues that occur on the internal level, but now let's consider what may occur on the external level. In the case above with Altegrity and their USIS division we saw where their main customer (the US government) lost confidence in them and terminated their contracts. But what if your main customers are consumers? How do consumers react to hearing about these breaches and will they find another company to do business with?

The Ponemon Institute conducted a survey[37] focusing specifically on consumer reactions to a breach where their PII was compromised. Here are a few of the most interesting findings:

- 59% of the respondents said either they will discontinue their relationship with the company or they are less likely to have a relationship.
- 54% said that it didn't matter what the company did, e.g., sincerely apologize, offer credit monitoring, discounted products and services, etc., they would not do business again with that company.

In a separate survey by The Brunswick Group,[38] consumers expressed considerable worry around data breaches and stated that the breached organization should be held fiscally responsible for anything that happens to consumers as a result. Key findings from this survey include:

- 94% of consumers surveyed are concerned about retail data breaches.

---

37. Consumer Study on Aftermath of a Breach,
http://www.ponemon.org/local/upload/file/Consumer%20Study%20on%20Aftermath%20of%20a%20Breach%20FINAL%202.pdf
38. Main Street vs. Wall Street: Who is to blame for data breaches?,
https://www.brunswickgroup.com/publications/surveys/data-breach-survey/

- Consumers are nearly as likely to hold retailers responsible for data breaches as the criminals themselves. Only 34% blame the banks that issue debit and credit cards.
- 75% believe that retailers are not doing enough to prevent infiltrations into their customer data and payment systems.
- 70% of respondents believe that retailers should be held financially responsible for consumer losses that result from a breach, not banks or card issuers.
- Finally, and most troubling, 34% of those surveyed report that they no longer shop at a specific retailer due to a past data breach issue.

There is a bit of good news, though. Stock prices following a breach will only drop on average about 10-15% for a large enterprise, and could rebound in as little as 2-3 quarters. For smaller businesses, it could take a year or longer for the stock value to fully rebound. If you are a large enterprise and can weather the storm of stock devaluation and loss of one third of your customer base, then you will be fine… at least from a stock valuation perspective.

However, as shareholders you might want to look beyond only the short-term impact to your stock valuation and consider other factors that can significantly impact the organization's profitability, such as cash flow, legal fees, class action lawsuits, regulatory fines, and executive dismissals as we have described earlier in this chapter. If you are a small to medium size business, all of these factors can be egregious enough to force the company into bankruptcy. The losses can come from every direction.

After reviewing this chapter, you should have a much better understanding of the impact of a breach on an organization. It is not a one size fits all set of circumstances, and any one ancillary effect of a breach could lead to total loss. There should be no doubt in your minds that together we must get started right away on building a comprehensive cyber security program.

In the next chapter we will discuss how to build a rock-solid program.

Chapter 5:
Protecting Your Business: *Creating a Rock-Solid Program*

Cyber security is critical to the success of any organization. More and more Boards of Directors and Executive Leaders are realizing that they must have a comprehensive cyber security program in place to reduce the level of potential risk an organization may face. Without a comprehensive cyber security program, it exposes that same organization to a significantly higher level of enterprise and financial exposure. Boards and Executive Leaders need to have a better understanding of the risk, the legal implications of cyber risk, and the full financial impact a security breach can have on an organization as a whole. The truth is that a cyber-breach does not impact just one facet of a business. It can literally bring the entire company to its knees.

Pre-Planning Your Program

The intent of this chapter is to guide you through the steps you can take to build a rock solid cyber security program. These prohibitive measures are effective, regardless of the size of your organization, or the risk level of your particular business and industry. Depending on the size of your business, you can take these resources and then scale the size of your program. There is not a one-size-fits-all solution. Each business will have unique risks, different threats and vulnerabilities, and specific levels of risk tolerance. This chapter will provide you with the guidelines to help you prioritize your cyber security investments to maximize each dollar spent. How you implement these guidelines will vary. But ultimately, this chapter is designed to help you better reduce and manage the cyber security threats faced by your business.

Some initial questions that may surface are:

Where do we begin?

What are the first steps we should take before we actually implement or upgrade the organized structure of our cyber security program?

With those in mind, the following steps will answer those questions and begin your journey to create a rock solid cyber security program:

1. Make a Decision

The first step is to actually make a decision. You must make the decision to develop and implement a world-class cyber security program. World-class doesn't mean a big financial commitment. It means having a cyber security program that understands the business, the risk to the business, your risk tolerance, and takes the necessary steps using people, processes, and technology that provides comprehensive cyber security protection. As Don Shula, NFL Hall of Fame Coach said, "The start is what stops most people." Decisions on cyber security, or the lack thereof, are responsible for the making or breaking of many a business. Executive leaders, who have become very proficient at making business decisions, often fall short in making the proper decisions related to cyber security.

2. Hire a Rock Star!

The C-level executive responsible for building your world-class cyber security program is the Chief Information Security Officer (CISO). If you don't yet have a CISO in your organization, it must be a top priority to create the position and hire into it. To be the most effective to the business, the CISO should be properly positioned in the organizational structure. Unfortunately, too many organizations bury the CISO two or more levels below where he/she should be and thereby unintentionally marginalize the position. Inevitably, the program suffers because of it. Ideally, the CISO should report to the CEO, but no lower than the COO, as the CISO must have direct access to the other C-level executives in the organization, and regular access to the COO, CEO, and Board of Directors. Having the CISO report to a position lower than the COO reduces the CISO's level of authority and complicates his/her gaining easy direct access to these other executives, as the CISO will not be on their same level.

There are three types of CISOs:

1. Those who are very technical but lack in both people and executive management skills.

2. Those who are very good in policy, governance, and executive presentations, but weak on technical skills.

3. Those CISOs who have a very strong technical knowledge and also excel in executive program management. They are your leaders, visionaries, and top tier CISOs. They are also few and far between.

As you can tell, the third category is the one in which your rock stars fall. And that is for whom you should be gunning. If you want a rock solid program, you need a rock star to lead it. But where do you find the leader of the band?

To find your rock star, it would be advantageous to use an executive recruiting agency that is experienced in hiring top tier CISOs. In most organizations, the talent acquisition managers do not understand the knowledge, skills, and abilities required for a CISO. Understanding these prerequisites goes far beyond comparing resumes to position descriptions. Retained executive recruiting agencies specialize in understanding the backgrounds and experience of CISOs, and are experts in screening candidates to provide you with the available cream of the crop. It is worth the investment. Keep in mind that it could take between 3–6 months from the time you create the position description to the time your new CISO begins. You also might want to consider hiring a consultant on a 3 to 6-month contract to serve as your Interim CISO.

In the next chapter we will describe in great detail the role and responsibilities of the CISO.

3. Conduct a Strategic Cyber Security Assessment

While you are working on hiring your CISO, it would be beneficial to contract a security-consulting firm to conduct a strategic cyber security assessment of your organization. Evaluation leads to improvement. Your CISO would want to do this anyway, so save the time and get started. When the CISO starts he/she can hit the ground running, provided you contract a reputable firm with Fortune 500 experience. The strategic assessment will determine the current security posture of the organization, where you need to be, and provide a recommended strategic plan of how to get there. The CISO will validate the plan and make any necessary adjustments once he/she begins.

A comprehensive cyber security program begins with implementing baseline standards such as the National Institute of Standards and Technology (NIST) Cyber Security Risk Management Framework. By leveraging and implementing a proven framework, it provides the starting point in building an all-inclusive program to protect systems and detect potential problems. The strategic cyber security assessment should be based on the NIST cyber security risk management framework, or other similar internationally accepted framework.

4. Budget Fiscal Resources

Organizations must fully understand the financial downside of underfunding cyber security. The cyber security program cannot be successful without the proper allocation of resources, both fiscal and human. The first step is creating a budget for the cyber security department. This budget is completely separate from the IT budget. I recommend making the CISO responsible for the P&L of the department, as any other business leader in the company is responsible for their own budget. The CISO also must be able to understand and plan for CAPEX and OPEX, and building strong business cases for each investment. For your initial planning for the cyber security program budget, the CFO can plan on an amount that is approximately 10 to 14% of the IT budget. The actual amount will depend upon the current level of program maturity. If you have a mature program already in place, then your budget could fall in the 5-9% range of the IT budget. With the proper security architecture and engineering, and procurement of leading-edge technology, your CISO should be able to reduce resource expenditures in future years once the amount of business risk is reduced to an acceptable level.

5. Managing the Human Element

Along with the fiscal resources, you will need to plan for managing the human capital for your cyber security team. You cannot rely on technology alone. You need highly-trained technicians to run the technology, interpret and analyze the data, dig into any possible anomalies, and respond immediately to events. Finding and hiring experienced cyber security personnel is quite challenging. We will discuss these challenges in the next section; however, equally important as hiring personnel is working to retain them. You must plan and budget for training, education, and a career growth path for these personnel, otherwise you face the risk of losing them to better offers elsewhere. Replacing experienced personnel is expensive when you factor in things like advertising, recruiters (if you use an external agency), interviewing, background investigations, the down time for the vacant position, and the vulnerability that being short-handed presents.

6. Insource or Outsource

Building out your cyber security program to include a fully staffed 24x7 Security Operations Center can be expensive. As many businesses look to cut costs in order to increase profitability, outsourcing security might initially appear to be a cost effective move. However, if it is not done properly, it can provide a false sense of security and end up being extremely costly to your business.

The main reason organizations outsource their security is because they do not want to invest in the people, processes, and technologies required to build their own capability. The tools can be quite expensive, and the headcount, which includes pay and benefits, can be equally as expensive. Managed Security Service Providers (MSSP) offer security for your company at what appears to be a better value, and in some cases it can be. This would make a lot of sense for a small to medium size business. You probably only have a couple of data centers, a couple of Internet points of presence, and can feed all your data to them for less cost than you could building out your own security infrastructure.

However, if you are a large enterprise, using an MSSP might not be your best option. Large enterprises usually have complex network infrastructures, data centers located around the world, and sensitive business information and intellectual property that you don't really want to outsource. The idea of outsourcing your risk might seem good at first, but MSSPs primarily look at what is coming in and out of a network (potential attack points) and a few other areas. Thus, they will be limited in providing you blanket security against all potential threats.

There are two other main areas of concern with outsourcing. The first is quality. MSSPs will normally have excellent technologies and well-practiced, documented processes. The challenge comes in with the people. In a large multi-tenant environment, MSSP analysts are watching the alerts of many different companies. They do not have the same level of passion that an internal analyst would have looking at alerts within his/her own organization. MSSP analysts normally won't go digging into the haystack to find the needle, whereas your own analysts would. Passion and drive is what saves companies.

Which leads right into the second area, which is Incident Response. This is another a la carte item, and some MSSPs don't have it on their menu despite it being the most important item of all in security. The last thing your head of security or other risk executive wants is a phone call at 2 AM that says, "It looks like you have a problem and might be breached" without the next words being, "and our Incident Response Team will be on the ground first thing in the morning." Isn't that why you outsource? You don't have the resources to do it yourself? So make sure you contract for Incident Response.

When making your decision to insource or outsource, consider the following:

- Cost – Are the initial lower costs actually worth outsourcing the risk management of your crown jewels? Make sure you do a detailed long-term cost benefit analysis.

- Incident Response – Whether or not you outsource, incident response should be one of your highest cyber security priorities. Make sure you establish detailed Service Level Agreements (SLA) with your MSSP for incident response if you are breached or they are breached.

- Services and Architecture – Determine what services the MSSP will provide. Your business is not safe unless you have security monitoring of all aspects of the business. If the MSSP cannot cover all these areas, then will you have to develop an internal capability for these services? How does that factor into the cost? Remember, it's not just monitoring your corporate networks. You might have data in the cloud.

- Global or Domestic – If you do not have international locations, then an MSSP who is domestic only is fine; however, if you do have international locations then clearly understand how the MSSP will support your international operations 24x7x365. Regardless of the time of day or where in the world you are operating, you want the A-Team monitoring your systems and data.

- Requests for Proposals – Have a bake off! Have your CISO, or your security consultant, put together a detailed RFP for monitoring and then review all the responses. Then have the top 3 or 4 vendors come in for an on-site presentation and Q&A to compare each.

There's not a one size fits all solution with the decision to in- or outsource. Each MSSP is different and each organization is different. After going through the steps above you might come to the decision, as I have in my organizations, that you do not want to outsource your risk management. You might also consider a hybrid. You might outsource some monitoring and perform some in house. Or, you might outsource initially and have the MSSP assist you in building an in house capability over the next 2–3 years that will, over time, phase the MSSP out and bring your security in house.

7. Organizing the Cyber Security Team

You've created a CISO position working for the CEO or COO. You've decided that you do not want to outsource your risk so you've allocated fiscal resources for the technologies you will need. The last thing you need to understand is how many people you will actually need to execute your rock solid cyber security program. That number is going to be different for every organization and is dependent on your size, geographic locations, and risk appetite. Rather than provide you with specific headcount numbers, as they will vary from organization to organization, let me list the specific areas of responsibility for which your cyber security team must address. The major functional areas are listed here. I will explain them in more detail in Section III below.

- Monitoring
- Incident Response
- Security Architecture & Engineering
- Compliance and Governance
- Policy & Training
- Project Management

There are many other functional areas of responsibility that the cyber security team works. However, if you develop an organizational structure that supports the above six areas, your team can also support all the other functional areas effectively. You now have the baseline for your rock solid cyber security program and are ready for the next steps.

The Hiring Process

Whether you consider it or not, the hiring process is one of the hardest parts of building a rock solid cyber security program. When I have built global cyber security programs in or for organizations, one my biggest challenges was in hiring experienced, high-quality team members. It is also the most time consuming portion of building your program.

As I stated earlier, the best approach to hiring a rock star CISO is to retain and use an external recruiting firm who is experienced in recruiting CISOs for Fortune 500 companies. They know exactly what qualities make an outstanding CISO and usually have a rolodex of the top CISOs in the country. You need only to provide the position description and ballpark compensation range to position them to quickly begin work. They will do all the pre-screening, and the candidates you see are going to be high quality.

Most of the other hires for your cyber security team will be done by your CISO. Remember: rock star analysts want to work for rock star CISOs! Once you get a few rock star analysts, they attract others, as well as feed off one another and continue to make themselves even better. Before you know it, you have a whole team of rock stars!

Generally, there are two levels of positions:

1. Managerial Experts – Managers will be those running the functional areas (described above)
2. Subject Matter Experts – These will be your analysts (described below)

Your subject matter experts could include positions such as:

- **SOC Cyber Security Analyst** – personnel who are experienced working within a 24x7 SOC. Recommend you hire people with experience using the toolsets you have or will have
- **Cyber Threat Intel Analysts** – for these you will probably have a few different position descriptions to cover experience in cyber threat intelligence collection and analysis, forensics, incident response, and malware reverse engineering
- **Cyber Security Engineer/Architect** – these positions will require experience in network engineering, security architecture, network infrastructure, active directory, and much more
- **Security Compliance Analysts** –finding personnel who have experience as security auditors or automated electronic governance systems will be very helpful
- **Policy Writer** – you want experience specifically writing cyber security policies and SOPs
- **Training Manager** – expertise in creating cyber security training & awareness programs, developing awareness bulletins and campaigns, and developing internal training programs for your cyber defenders

A shortage of cyber security professionals has been an issue for many years. However, this issue continues to grow exponentially with the advent of more and more sophisticated attacks resulting in major breaches to organizations. Recently, Michael Brown, CEO of security vendor Symantec, stated, "The demand for the (cyber security) workforce is expected to rise to 6 million (globally) by 2019, with a projected shortfall of 1.5 million"[39]. According to a Peninsula Press analysis[40] of numbers from the US Bureau of Labor Statistics, in early 2015 more than 209,000 cyber security jobs in the U.S. were unfilled, and job postings were up 74 percent over the previous five years. The demand for cyber security professionals is expected to grow by 53 percent through 2018.

With this shortage, try not to make the recruiting of these professionals harder than it is. When you are creating your position descriptions, be careful what you consider mandatory prerequisites vs. desired, or more accurately – necessity vs. luxury.

For example, when hiring your subject matter experts, the need for a Bachelor's degree is not necessary; it's nice to have. In today's world, we see high school age, and even younger, people who are expert hackers and know technology very well. Experience is what you need in your subject matter experts and analysts.

Remember, you will to have compensate these cyber security subject matter experts more than you would an IT engineer or IT analyst. Just get it in your mind now. If you want a rock solid program, you will have to pay above market rates, particularly in this high demand, low supply field. And that is assuming your potential candidate is local. Always remember there may be an occasion where you have to look outside of your city, state, or even region to find the best fit for your business. Of course that would come with relocation costs, and sometimes a signing bonus. Either way, the most important thing to consider is who would be the best fit, from both an experience and personality perspective, to ensure you are moving your organization in the right direction.

Executing the Game Plan

With a strong game plan in place, this is where the rubber meets the road. In addition to creating the CISO position and providing the CISO with the

---

39. Cybersecurity's Labor Epidemic, http://www.forbes.com/sites/stevemorgan/2015/09/21/%E2%80%8Bcybersecuritys-labor-epidemic/
40. Demand to Fill Cybersecurity Jobs Booming, http://peninsulapress.com/2015/03/31/cybersecurity-jobs-growth/

necessary resources to either build a comprehensive internal program, or to outsource a large portion of it, it is essential that cyber security is one of the organization's top strategic goals. The CISO, in building the program, will develop rapport and relationships with the executive leaders of Legal, Compliance, HR, IT, Corporate Communications, Physical Security, the various lines of business, and others, as needed. They will communicate regularly, whether formally or informally, to review and discuss the strategic goals of the business and how the cyber security program is supporting them.

Functional Areas

Let's first take a look at each of the major areas of responsibility of the cyber security program that I listed earlier. There are some areas where your team members can be dual-hatted and work more than one specific area of responsibility. I will indicate where this might be possible. Keep in mind though that when you pull from one area you may weaken another.

1. Monitoring

Whether you insource or outsource, you must have 24x7x365 monitoring of all your networks, systems, and data. I have gone into organizations who, for cost reduction reasons, had monitoring 12x5; basically Monday–Friday 7 AM to 7 PM. This is like hanging a sign up on the front door of the company at the end of the day saying please don't breach us tonight, we will be back in the morning. The attackers operate 24x7, so shouldn't you?

2. Incident Response

Within cyber security, incident response is the most important area of all. There is always the potential to be breached even with a rock solid program. The difference is that a rock solid program has a great incident response plan and will contain an incident quickly and prevent egregious harm to an organization. This is one area where you should consider a dual role for these team members. While it is possible for your IR team to come from the SOC analysts, I normally prefer not to do that. If your SOC is investigating a security attack, and your analysts are also your incident responders, then you have to pull them from monitoring the network to respond to an incident whereby they would miss seeing new attacks or activity. I like to have my incident responders separate from my SOC analysts. Where I dual-hat them is as cyber threat intelligence analysts. When they are not responding to incidents, they are collecting and analyzing cyber threat intelligence from all sources.

3. Security Architecture & Engineering

This team is invaluable in reducing risk inside the organization. They work very closely with IT and the business units on all existing and future products. They will evaluate applications, websites, research & development projects, 3rd party remote access, changes to firewalls, routers, infrastructure, and anything else that will potentially expose a network to risk. They will determine the level of security risk and work with the project owner to find a secure solution. They will also conduct research and development, and the testing of new security tools and technologies to make sure they remain current and applicable to the evolving threat.

4. Compliance and Governance

This team is responsible for ensuring the IT regulatory compliance of the organization. However, they are more like auditors than hands-on implementers. They have oversight for all IT compliance and regulatory requirement activities. They conduct audits to ensure compliance with policy, security controls, and regulatory requirements. They work closely with internal audit departments, regulators, and provide support to external auditors.

5. Policy & Training

This team is responsible for cyber security policy development and also your cyber security-training program. They conduct annual reviews and updates of policy, as well as develop cyber security SOPs that support those same policies. They also develop and implement training and awareness programs for all employees, which would include annual online training, regular email alerts, and education, as well as individual training of cyber security staff.

6. Project Management

This last team is especially important for larger enterprises. The cyber security team is involved in almost all new and ongoing projects in the organization and supporting the business. Consequently, it is very helpful to the business and the cyber security team to have Project Managers who can track all ongoing projects in order to help keep them on time and on budget, at least from a cyber security support perspective. These PMs also should have in-depth cyber security knowledge and experience, and be capable of sitting with IT engineers and discussing the projects intelligently.

The above six areas are the main stress points for your cyber security program. It is not an all-inclusive list of areas of responsibility. These are the major groups. However, using the above areas as a guide, you can develop the organizational structure for your cyber security program. Then, under these functional areas you will have personnel who perform all the other smaller, yet equally important tasks within cyber security. Now let's look at another very important aspect of cyber security.

Business Integration

To close this chapter, it is important to note the connection between cyber security and the role it plays in your overall organization. A key component of any rock solid cyber security program is integration with your business. To this point, you now know that cyber risk is a business risk and not an IT function. In years past, cyber security focused on locking down users' computers and often didn't really have much insight into business operations or risks. A lot of this is attributed to the fact that cyber security was buried in the organizational structure and was significantly under-funded. That has now changed. Rock star CISOs understand the business. They understand the business risk and the risk appetite of the business. They have built rapport with the executive leaders, and the CISO knows exactly what they need to protect (the crown jewels of each line of business) and how to do so, while allowing the business to be innovative and its employees more productive. Because your rock star has built, or is building a world-class program, cyber security is now being integrated in business decision-making.

Effectively folding cyber security into business processes allows your executive management team to make better risk management decisions on business investments and operations. The strategic focus has shifted to where cyber security investments support enterprise business risk management decisions for the entire organization.

To recap, my hope is that you have now hired a rock star CISO.

- ✓ He/she is reporting to the CEO and presenting to the Board of Directors at each meeting. You have decided to insource the entire program.

- ✓ With the resources you have authorized and the authority granted to the CISO, your program was built.

- ✓ You have a 24x7 Security Operations Center that is monitoring and responding to events and engaging incident response whenever anything looks even remotely suspicious.

- ✓ The CISO has built relationships with the executives running your lines of business. They are very happy knowing that there is a personal interest in supporting them and allowing them to be more innovative and productive, all while keeping their crown jewels secure.

- ✓ You have leading-edge security technology that has significantly reduced your level of business risk while raising your security profile without hindering business operations at all.

- ✓ Your compliance programs are meeting all regulatory compliance requirements.

- ✓ Your cyber insurance provider has reduced the annual rate because your program is demonstrably rock solid.

Your colleagues in other businesses and organizations are asking you how you accomplished this. Your response: "I made the decision and followed through on it."

In the next chapter we are going to look in depth at the role and responsibility of the CISO to gain a greater understanding of how difficult this position is and why it is so critical to the success of your business.

Chapter 6:

Leading the Charge: *The Role and Responsibilities of a CISO*

As evidenced in previous chapters, cyber security is critical to the success of your organization. More and more Boards of Directors and Executive Leaders are realizing that they must have a comprehensive cyber security program in place to reduce the level of risk and prevent a catastrophic outcome. Remember, the Chief Information Security Officer (CISO) is the C-level executive responsible for cyber security within your organization. The CISO should report to the CEO to be most effective to the business. However, in very large enterprises it might work to have the CISO report to the COO. With that said, having the CISO report to a position lower than the COO reduces the CISO's level of authority and complicates his/her ability to gain easy and direct access to these other executives, as the CISO will not be on their same level.

Although the CISO is typically identified closely with Information Technology (IT), the CISO's cyber security organization is fundamentally different than IT. The IT department is primarily responsible for the operation and maintenance of the organization's networks, systems, applications, technology development, and communications systems. They provide technological solutions for the business, but they are not a security organization. The CISO's team is responsible for ensuring that all technology services and solutions are safe and properly secured. It is the CISO's responsibility to then make sure the level of risk is aligned to the risk appetite of the business, as determined by the board and executive leadership.

Rock Star Qualities

Now that you know cyber security is a top priority, the next step is to hire that rock star CISO. That said, what are the qualities that make him/her stand out enough to be considered a rock star in cyber security? You'll find those below:

- **Leadership** – your CISO must be an outstanding leader who leads by example, remains calm, and has an even temperament. Spencer Stuart, an executive search and leadership consulting firm, draws on their extensive research to identify several key leadership traits and skills.[41] These include:
  - Exceptional business judgment
  - The ability to recognize interpersonal dynamics and apply them in decision making
  - Highly effective people management and team building
  - Humility and substance
  - Effective people development skills
  - The ability to drive change

- **Strategic Thinker** – your CISO must be able to bridge the gap between technology, cyber security, and the needs of the business. He/she must be able to see the big picture and generate ideas and solutions that solve security challenges while also supporting the business mission.

- **Great Communicator** – your CISO must be able to effectively communicate with a wide variety of audiences. He/she must be able to translate technical language into business speak when communicating with business leaders, senior executives, and board directors. He/she should be able to understand and speak in-depth technically with IT personnel and vendors. And yet also be able to translate into another language when speaking with employees and the general public while representing the company publicly.

- **Technologist** – your CISO must thoroughly understand threats, vulnerabilities, risk, the exploitation of systems, and how technologies can protect a network. They must be able to discuss intelligently at a technical level with IT engineers and security analysts.

---

41. Understanding Executive Potential, https://www.spencerstuart.com/research-and-insight/understanding-executive-potential-the-underappreciated-leadership-traits

- **Expert Crisis Manager** – ideally your CISO will have been through major business crises where they were responsible for leading their teams through the crisis. In the event of a major breach, the CISO must be able to calmly and effectively lead an executive crisis action team while simultaneously leading the incident response.

- **Team Builder** – your CISO must be able to establish rapport and build relationships with key business leaders and executives within your organization, as well as build and lead his/her own cyber security team.

- **Problem Solver** – your CISO must have a keen ability to see beyond symptoms and determine the root cause of problems, develop multiple courses of action in line with business priorities, evaluate them, and then implement the best solution.

Not all CISO candidates will have an equal amount of all these traits. However, the more they have of each one, the closer you will be to finding your rock star.

According to Mr. Bruce Brody, former CISO for the US Department of Veterans Affairs, US Department of Energy, and Fortune 500 companies, "The CISO has an organizational transformation role, with strong hooks into IT, Risk, HR, GC, Physical Security and the entire enterprise, top to bottom. Creating a risk-conscious and security-aware culture across the enterprise should be the first priority of a CISO. Maintaining a risk-conscious and security-aware culture across the enterprise should be the second priority of a CISO."

The Responsibilities of a CISO

Now let's look at some of the major responsibilities of a CISO. The following is a summary of the major responsibilities, which is followed by a detailed explanation of each.

- Security Assessments
- Risk Management
- Policy and Governance
- Security Architecture and Engineering

- Security Monitoring
- Incident Response
- Cyber Threat Intelligence
- Forensics

Security Assessments

One of the CISO's first and most important responsibilities is to conduct an overall cyber security assessment, including an analysis of the cyber security readiness of the organization. The analysis by the CISO, or a third party security consultant, will include identifying gaps in the organization's cyber security operations, security organizational structure, and any significant vulnerabilities that may expose the business to significant risk. As an outcome of identifying these gaps, the CISO will develop a Strategic Plan and a roadmap to improve the organization's readiness and operations for cyber security, and recommend the technologies, processes, and services to achieve such results. The CISO will further build and operationalize a full cyber security program on a timeline and budget the company can accommodate.

As an example of how important this responsibility is, when I was hired into one of my earliest CISO positions, I conducted a detailed security assessment shortly after starting in the position. I discovered during my assessment that an advanced persistent threat was on our network. The incident response and forensics investigation revealed that they were on the network for nearly 6 months, which is consistent with the average dwell time an advanced threat is on a network from breach to discovery. It cost the company ten million dollars to mitigate and rebuild. Do you know if anyone is on your network?

The CISO must evaluate the current security resources within the organization and make recommendations to right size the cyber security team to make sure that the organization has the correct number of resources to be successful. It's not necessarily just a numbers game. Larger cyber security teams do not necessarily equate to a higher level of security. An analysis of the existing resources must be done. The CISO must look within the company and see who is currently performing cyber security tasks.

Are they in the IT department, another business unit, or within the cyber security department? If they are outside the cyber security department, are they dedicated 100% to performing security tasks, or are they dual-hatted performing other IT functions such as being a system or network administrator, a help desk technician, a data base administrator, or some other function? Are the existing personnel, whether within the cyber security department or elsewhere, trained, qualified, and capable of effectively performing security tasks and functions?

Risk Management

The CISO provides leadership, vision, management, and support to the organization's cyber security program through developing and leading programs and processes to monitor the emergence of new threats and vulnerabilities, assessing impacts and driving responses as appropriate. He/she then ensures that clear and timely business advice is provided to executive management on key cyber security and assurance issues to help establish a global cyber security and risk management capability and architecture across the organization. He/she also ensures that cyber security and risk are adequately represented on relevant business and governance forums and is known, well-integrated, and well-respected across the enterprise.

In 2009, Scott Goodhart joined AES Corporation, a Fortune 200 and world leading power generation company. He is currently serving as Vice President, Global Network and CISO. In this role, he oversees the operations of the AES global network and is responsible for cyber security issues and securing digital information. Scott's prior assignment was Vice President, Global IT Infrastructure, and he was responsible for the operations of the AES global data centers and the email platform.

When asked what he thinks are the most important responsibilities of a CISO, Goodhart replied, "One of the CISO's most important responsibilities is to be able to clear the Fog of Cyber and explain cyber risk as business risk. Doing this in a way without resorting to FUD (Fear, Uncertainty, and Doubt) goes a long way in building credibility with business leaders."

Cyber Insurance

Another important area of risk management is determining whether or not you need cyber breach insurance, and if so, the suggested amount. Some insurance companies refer to it as cyber liability insurance, and others might call it data breach insurance. Regardless of the name, the goal of insurance is to transfer some of the residual risks and costs your organization may incur as the result of a cyber security breach. However, there will be millions of dollars in costs to the company that can severely strain financial resources. More often than not the breach losses are much higher than anticipated. You will have to decide how to manage this risk, how much you can accept, and how much you should transfer via cyber insurance.

Cyber insurance is a relatively new concept, offered first to the general public and organizations in the early 90's. That said, there aren't any internationally accepted standards yet. This means every policy will vary from insurance company to insurance company to include the exclusions. When selecting a carrier and a policy, it is important that you carefully review all aspects to determine what you require. Do not accept policies with unreasonable exclusions, or in other words, those policies that exclude what security experts would consider a probable type of attack on a company such as by a nation state.

According to an Internet Security Alliance[42] report on the financial management of cyber risk, superior cyber risk policies should provide the following coverage:

- Third-party litigation and regulatory investigations (especially those arising from theft of personally identifiable information) including legal expenses, judgments, and settlements
- First-party losses an insured company may suffer from business interruption, and "extra expenses" incurred due to a covered cyber security event

---

42. www.isalliance.org, The Financial Management of Cyber Risk

- With respect to PII theft events, enhanced coverage for crisis management expenses, state notification expenses, and other remediation costs

As for exclusions, often you will see exclusions for the following:

- Failing to meet minimum security requirements/implementing industry best practices
- Failing to provide the insurer notification of a material change to information provided in the application
- Breach representation or warranties made in the application
- Breaches conducted by terrorists or nation state attackers

As you can see, you will still need to build a rock solid cyber program even with cyber insurance. Bullets two and three under exclusions refer to how you represent your company in the application. If you state you have a solid cyber security program and have the policies and procedures in place to support it, and then are later breached, it is possible the insurance company's separate investigation could determine that you actually didn't satisfy their requirements, or the technologies and policies were far out of date, resulting in non-payment by the insurance company. The last exclusion you cannot accept, as nation state attackers are the biggest threat to all businesses.

The cost of a cyber insurance policy varies from organization to organization and carrier to carrier depending on the coverage, limits, and retention. It could cost less than $1,000 a year for small to medium size businesses. For large enterprises, the cost could be over a million dollars per year.

Policy and Governance: Auditor Not Implementer

The CISO's team will develop the required security policies in compliance with regulatory requirements, and internal business needs. The policies are coordinated with legal, HR, and IT to ensure they are legally sound and can be implemented and enforced. The policies establish a governance baseline for the cyber security program.

Policies, like all other security controls, must be properly enforced. As you consider the difference between IT and cyber security, think of the IT teams as the implementers and the cyber security team as the regulators. The implementers are the ones who are hands-on and make the changes to the system. The CISO is the auditor who makes sure the changes are secure and in compliance with the regulatory requirements. The auditors are the ones who establish the standards, approve any deviations or exceptions to the standards, and conduct audits to ensure that the established standards are being met. It is for this reason that there needs to be a separation of roles. The auditors must be separate from the implementers. Security should never be overruled to meet a production deadline or other similar reason.

For example, consider if your company has a new promotion for an upcoming event or sale. The IT developers create a new web application for the event. The developers, rushing to meet a deadline, do not properly test their code. The CIO directs his team to go live with the new application to meet the business timeline. Keep in mind that malicious actors are scanning your public facing websites every single day. If a malicious actor is targeting your company, then there will be regular in depth scans on all your company websites. Once the attacker finds this new web application, they will attack every part of it looking for vulnerability. Once found, the vulnerability is then exploited and the attacker is able to gain access to the network. The next step is to gain control of the main servers that run your networks where they steal all usernames and passwords in the company. They now have the keys to the kingdom. Game over. Business compromised.

Security Architecture and Engineering

It is important that the CISO has a team that includes security engineers and architects. The specific number depends on the size of the organization. If it is a large global company, then you might have one or two in each geographic area of operations. If it's a small to mid-size company, then you might have only a single person who performs both roles. The CISO makes sure that his team works very closely with IT and the business units on all existing and future projects. They will evaluate applications, websites, research and development projects, third party remote access, changes to firewalls, routers, infrastructure, and anything else that will potentially expose a network to risk. The bottom line is that the CISO's team must review all changes to the network from an engineering and architectural perspective to ensure the proposed changes do not create a vulnerability that was not previously there.

There might be some acceptable duplicity in performing security tasks. For example, the IT department will typically have network engineers who manage the firewalls. These are the team members who would typically make changes to the firewalls, edit Access Control Lists, troubleshoot, and perform upgrades, other maintenance, and these types of tasks. These personnel should remain within the IT department. However, the CISO has oversight of them because the firewalls are security tools. No changes are made to any firewall or other security device without the review and approval of the CISO or his/her designated representative. All changes must be reviewed for impact to security architecture and engineering, and approved by the CISO designated representative before they can be made.

Security Monitoring

Another very important responsibility for the CISO is to monitor network traffic. The CISO, and his team, should consider the information and data that is flowing in, out of, and across the network. Today's threat landscape has changed significantly and the malicious actors are very good at surreptitiously gaining access to the network, remaining hidden in plain sight, moving laterally around the network to conduct reconnaissance, collecting intellectual property, trade secrets, customer and employee information and other sensitive business data, then transmitting that data out of the network. The CISO must have specialized tools in place that monitor the flow of information coming into the network via the Internet, email, removable media, or other sources. This monitoring must be 24x7x365 whether the CISO builds out an internal Security Operations Center or manages the outsourcing to a Managed Security Services Provider.

Incident Response

One of, if not THE most important responsibilities for the CISO is Incident Response (IR). An organization could spend millions of dollars in cyber security tools and technologies, but the organization can still be breached if they are not the right technologies. Consequently, a rock solid incident response program is absolutely necessary. The incident response team needs to be able to respond to an incident within minutes of detection; not hours, days, weeks, or months. The CISO must develop a documented and detailed IR plan. The company executives, not just the IR Team, must train on the IR plan. Start small with table top exercises within the cyber security department with small event simulations, then expand it to include the IT department, then eventually expand it to include a semi-annual event that includes business and C-Suite executives. The same way you are supposed to train annually on Disaster Recovery (DR) and Continuity of Operations (COOP), but must organizations don't, you MUST have training annually that includes everyone who would be involved in a real breach.

When the organization is breached, the CISO must take the lead immediately and manage the incident. The severity of the breach determines the steps the CISO will need to take. If it is a major incident, the CISO will need to immediately form a Crisis Action Team (CAT). The CAT will include the CEO, COO, CFO, CIO, General Counsel, Corporate Communications (or public affairs) Officer, CHRO, and senior executives from the lines of business. The CAT will most likely meet three to four times a day immediately after discovery of the breach until such time as the incident is contained. Then the frequency of meetings will be reduced until the incident is mitigated. At the CAT meetings, the CISO will provide as much factual details on the breach as possible. Speculation should not be provided, except to describe the worst and best case scenarios. The CAT must determine what public statement(s) should be made and the timing of such statements. Notifications also need to be made to the Board of Directors, regulators, merchant banks, and others. These notifications also will be coordinated through the CAT. Whether or not federal law enforcement will be notified, or their assistance requested, will be determined by the CAT.

Cyber Threat Intelligence

Cyber threat intelligence is another important area of responsibility for the CISO. The cyber security teams must stay up to date on the latest threats, vulnerabilities, malware, and types of attacks. This information is extremely useful in confirming that the organization is properly prepared to defend against any new threats or methods of attack.

The CISO must sort through quite a few sources of threat intelligence information and select the ones that make the most sense for your organization. Some of these sources are from commercial companies who sell subscriptions to their threat databases and email distribution lists. Some also offer analyst services. If your team has questions about threat information, or possibly a piece of malware they discovered on the network, they can request analyst support from the company. Another good source of threat intelligence information is from an Information Sharing and Analysis Center (ISAC). These are industry specific organizations that usually charge a fee to join. The fee is often scaled based on the organization's annual revenue. Not every industry has an ISAC. At the time of this writing there are nineteen ISACs including Financial Services, Aviation, Health Care, Electricity, Transportation, and Supply Chain. There is also a Multi-State ISAC that is a collaborative group of states and local governments. The Defense Industrial Base also has its own ISAC.

In addition to commercial or fee-based threat intelligence centers, there are many free services. The FBI has an organization, Infragard, that is open to the public to join, following proper vetting and a background investigation. This is a good source of information not only on cyber threats, but physical security, as well. The Department of Homeland Security's United States Computer Emergency Readiness Team (US-CERT) provides updates on threat information and maintains a vulnerability database that provides detailed technical information on system vulnerabilities. Other government agencies also have web pages and distribution lists sharing cyber threat information. Carnegie Mellon University's Software Engineering Institute operates the CERT Division, which is one of the country's leading cyber security resources.

Forensics Investigations

CISOs are also responsible for forensics investigations. Not only is it necessary to have a forensics capability in support of a cyber security breach, but also forensics capability is necessary to support internal Legal and HR Department investigations. These latter requirements will most likely be needed quite more frequently than the former. There are a number of tools and technologies that can assist the CISO in being able to quickly acquire information that is required in support of an investigation. This is an area that requires well-defined, trained, and practiced processes and procedures, particularly in support of any legal actions. There must be a clearly defined chain of custody process that must be followed exactly so that evidence cannot be disallowed on a technicality in a court of law. The forensics team might need to be trained in multiple forensics platforms that legal practices use for file sharing.

A Day in the Life of a CISO

Sound like a lot of responsibilities? Well, the truth is that it takes a village to prevent a cyber breach, but it starts with the CISO and his/her everyday roles. A great CISO can make an enormous difference. That said, let's take a brief look at a day in the life of a CISO when not responding to or managing a security incident. While there really isn't a typical day, as events, projects, and meetings are constantly changing (being flexible is critical), here are some general guidelines and expectancies any CISO should consider.

The CISO is usually up before dawn. Before that first cup of coffee in the morning the CISO is checking email to see what came in since he/she went to bed just a few hours earlier. If there are no immediate fires to put out, the CISO will check in by phone with his/her team located in earlier time zones, e.g., Europe or east coast if the CISO is west coast based.

Once in the office, there is a morning meeting with his/her direct reports to get an update with where they are with various projects, see if there are any issues that he/she might need to weigh in on, and provide guidance for the day. The CISO will then check in on the SOC and see if they or the night shift saw anything of interest that they are digging into. If your CISO is a rock star, he/she also will walk through all of his/her team areas. The CISO needs to be visible and available to all team members. Depending on the number of business meetings on the CISO's calendar, which usually is very full, the CISO will swing by the IT department and stop in to see the CIO if he/she is available.

Throughout the day, a CISO will have meetings with vendors, business leaders, and strategic planning sessions with his security team leaders. In between, the CISO is working on strategic presentations for leadership and/or the board, reviewing security metrics, policies, and training newsletters. Additionally, the CISO is the final approving authority for changes to gateway firewalls, security architecture changes, or other changes that could impact the security of the organization.

In the late afternoon/early evening, the CISO is on teleconferences with his/her teams in Asia Pacific or time zones in the west. In the event of any security incidents, small or large, the CISO puts things on hold to investigate the event and work with his/her teams to determine the severity. Hopefully a CISO doesn't have a day where he/she is dealing with a head on breach. But the reality is that it is part of the job description. Those are often the most trying and difficult times for the CISO, as all hands are on deck and all eyes are on the captain of the ship. But that is what he/she signed up for. There is no greater need than during a cyber breach.

In this chapter, I have given you a glimpse of the major responsibilities of a CISO tasked with the enormous responsibility of leading the charge to protect your business. The list of responsibilities goes on and is quite extensive. Cyber security, and keeping your business secure, is a 24x7 operation and responsibility, which is why it requires a rock star CISO.

According to Brody, more and more Fortune 500 organizations are just now realizing that they truly require a rock star. "Almost a third of those companies don't have a true CISO, and another third believe a CISO is simply an IT security person who shouldn't be presenting in the C-Suite or the Board Room. The roughly one-third who "get it" are beginning to hire the true executive CISO, with a track record of success and a wealth of wisdom, able to stand toe-to-toe with corporate leadership and discharge the many challenging risk and compliance issues confronting the corporation."

It takes a rock star to be successful in keeping your business safe and preventing a breach. But if you should be breached, it'll take that same rock star to quickly contain it and mitigate before there is serious harm done.

In the next chapter we will discuss in detail how your rock star will manage and help your company recover from a breach.

Chapter 7:

Breach Management: *Recovering from the Carnage*

It is not a question of *if* your organization will be breached, but *when*. Despite all your best investment efforts into a cyber program, you find yourself hacked! Data security breaches leave organizations significantly exposed to operational, financial, and litigation risks. To survive a data breach, and potential post-breach litigation, organizations must have a two-part Incident Response Program:

1. The technical response handled by the CISO and his cyber security teams and

2. A well-planned and executed crisis management solution.

During a major breach, an effective program will bring order to a chaotic environment. And trust me, there will be chaos. The following is a good example of what it's like, and what you will need to do in this situation.

The Day of Dread

You hired your rock star CISO and empowered him/her by providing the resources to begin a deep dive assessment to determine the security profile of your organization. The CISO has procured the tools and team members needed to get the job done right. Late one evening, your Security Operations Center identifies some suspicious activity on the network. There is a large amount of data being moved from your servers and being consolidated onto a single workstation on the network. Data normally traverses across the network, but one of your rock star analysts thought it was a bit strange that this much data was going from a server to a workstation. Usually it's the other way around. The analyst started digging into this and found that the data moved to the workstation was split into much smaller encrypted files. The analyst immediately suspected that this looks like the way attackers access data from breached networks. Alarm bells are sounding!

During the breach, crisis management for the organization is performed through the CAT. The CAT is composed of the organization's senior executive leadership including the CEO, COO, CFO, CIO, CISO, General Counsel, CHRO, Chief Compliance Officer, and the Corporate Communications Officer. Lines of business leaders will be called or conferenced in as necessary. The CAT will provide guidance and expertise from the respective fields of each member, and make critical risk management decisions in a timely manner. The CAT is normally led by the CISO who is responsible for containing and eradicating the source of the breach, as well as providing regular updates to the CAT.

Key strategic questions the CAT should answer include:

1. How can we protect our employees and customers?
2. How can we minimize brand and reputation damage?
3. What are our reporting and notification requirements?
4. Should we notify and seek Law Enforcement assistance?
5. What are our operational, financial and litigation risks?
6. How can we shore up stakeholder trust?
7. What will the impact be on the organization in three, six, or twelve months' time?
8. Does this crisis present an opportunity to change the business and address underlying risks?

It's 2 AM and the CISO's cell phone rings. Unfortunately, CISOs' phones are never turned off or silenced at night. The CISO sees that it's the SOC calling and knows it's not good news. The SOC Chief, who was called back in a short while before, explains to the CISO what they've found. The CISO believes there is a strong chance that they have been breached. The SOC Chief described what is known as a staging server. This is where attackers centralize the data they are stealing, then break it up into small, encrypted files to send out of the network undetected. This is a critical stage at this point. The response must be immediate. The CISO directs the SOC Chief to do the following:

• Shut down all Internet connections for that network (thereby preventing any additional data from leaving the network).

- Initiate the cyber security team emergency recall roster (from that point until further notice they are operating in emergency mode 24x7).
- Do not use email to communicate regarding the breach. They must use an out of band communications method, e.g., cell phones, as the attacker most likely has compromised the email system and you don't want to tip them off that you are onto them.
- Locate the system the attacker is using as a staging server and run a forensics image (copy) of the system, then pull it off the network.
- Begin a deep dive malware scan of every system in the organization.

The CISO then notifies the CIO of the incident, and they will require IT's full attention and support in the investigation.

The CISO receives an update on the status upon arrival in the SOC. Details are sketchy; the attacker was very good at covering his or her tracks. From the initial loganalysis, they can see that three times a day only during peak business hours the compromised system would connect to Internet sites using https (encrypted Internet sessions, like if you were connecting to your bank), bypassing security monitoring. This too is another typical tactic used by attackers to blend in with normal daily activity and go unnoticed for months.

Confirmation of the breach

The CISO notifies the CEO and COO to inform them that the company was breached. They must stand up the Crisis Action Team (CAT) immediately. First meeting will be in the Executive Conference Room at 8:00 AM. Executives not physically available should dial in.

At the CAT meeting, the chaos begins. Questions are flying all around and the meeting hasn't yet begun. The CEO turns it over to the CISO who briefs the CAT on the situation – an unknown attacker breached the organization. It is too early to determine specifically what data has been taken at this point in the investigation. It appears the attacker was on the network for at least a couple of months and had access to all systems. We must prepare for the worst-case scenario. From the customer side, we have lost all PCI data on all past and present customers. We very well could have lost our Intellectual Property and possibly our R&D information as well. These two latter items will impact us significantly, but at a much later date. We need to plan now for how we are going to deal with the loss of customer information.

- First item on the agenda: do we engage federal law enforcement? The CISO's recommendation is yes, we need to contact our local FBI cyber security office. The CISO will coordinate and work directly with the FBI, but will keep the General Counsel informed on all communications and actions.

- Next, we need to prepare an initial public statement explaining we were the victim of an external malicious cyber attack, and some customer information may have been lost. We work closely with law enforcement and will provide more information as soon as it is available. Also, determine the timing of release of the statement.

- Notifications also need to be made to the Board of Directors, regulators, merchant banks, and others. Legal and Compliance also need to provide a list of to whom we must report and the associated timeline/reporting requirements.

- We should determine if we need to engage with external counsel who is experienced and well versed in the legal aspects of a cyber breach.

- Then, we should internally communicate to all our employees to advise them of the breach and tell them that they may not speak to anyone about the breach who is not a direct employee of the company. We need to limit and manage the details of the breach. Any information should only be released the Corporate Communications Officer.

- We will need to bring in a 3rd party breach containment and forensics vendor to assist our security teams in containing, mitigating, and conducting the detailed forensics examination. We might need a second vendor, if the primary is not certified as a PCI DSS Certified Forensics Investigator (CFI), which will be required by our merchant banks.

We should plan on reconvening this CAT every four hours over the next few days. We will reduce the frequency once we get the breach contained and have a better idea of what information was compromised.

The CISO then reaches out by phone to three of the top breach mitigation companies to determine which are immediately available, get rough cost estimates, quickly execute standard non-disclosure agreements, and determine if they are also PCI CFI certified. Based on the responses received, select a vendor. The CISO then meets with the CFO, GC, and senior procurement officer for funding and to put together a quick contract. Breach mitigation vendors do this all the time and can provide standard contract templates with Statements of Work designed specifically for Incident Response (IR). The CFO, GC, and procurement must execute the contract as quickly as they possibly can to ensure the vendor can deploy their initial IR team within 24 hours.

The CISO then reaches out to the local FBI office to brief them on the incident and solicit assistance. Depending on the size and scope of the breach, the FBI might create a joint task force that also includes the US Secret Service and other government agencies. They will combine their investigative resources and intelligence networks to see if they can find any information as to who conducted the attack, or if any malicious actors were trying to sell information on the Dark Web. They normally do not want any access to your network, but will ask for copies of log files and any malware that is found to provide their independent analysis.

Containment, Mitigation and Forensics

Your ability to effectively and quickly contain the breach depends in large part on the quality of your incident response program and the training of your team. Keep in mind that when a malicious actor breaches an organization, particularly if it's an advanced persistent threat, one of the first things that they do is to install multiple back doors (alternate ways to get into the network). In some cases, they put in "time bombs." These are malware that seem innocuous and appear to be normal system files. However, after a certain amount of time, a time bomb will wake up and phone home. It could be weeks, months, or even a year or more. So if you detect the breach and then mitigate it, but miss the hidden time bombs, the attacker could then breach the network again when they awake.

Containing the breach started when the CISO received the first call and directed his teams to shut down Internet access. This stops the bleeding, but can have a significant impact on business, particularly if you are hosting your own websites. But even a cloud-based host can be interrupted. Additionally, you cannot send or receive email, and depending on the type of email system you have, external personnel sending email to the company might see the email bounce and return to sender. Better designed systems will queue the email and deliver to the company once Internet connectivity is restored.

Be prepared to be without Internet access for several days. In most breaches, Internet connectivity is the first thing you cut off. Even with an excellent incident response plan and reacting very quickly, you will still lose Internet access for several days at most of your locations around the world. You might even be down for weeks at ground zero (the location of the main breach), as the entire network might need to be rebuilt.

Eventually, connectivity to these networks will be restored, as all systems on each network are thoroughly scanned and/or cleaned.

Mitigation is very challenging, particularly if your security teams and/or incident response vendor is unable to capture a piece of the malware or determine specifically how the attack was conducted. There is little hope if they cannot quickly analyze the files created or modified, the changes to system settings, and to where and what method the attacker used to communicate. This information is extremely helpful in locating additional compromised systems in your network.

The forensics investigation significantly helps in the containment, mitigation, and determination of the compromised data. Unfortunately, this is the hardest part of the incident response. Sophisticated attackers are extremely good at covering their tracks. They often will delete log files on systems so the incident responders do not know what systems they accessed, where they moved within the network, or what files and folders they accessed. Often times, it could take months to complete the forensics investigation even though full network and Internet connectivity is restored. One of the challenges is that the attackers encrypt the files before they send them out of your network. Even if you are fortunate enough to capture some of those files that were moved to a staging server, it is highly unlikely that you or your incident response vendor will be able to decrypt the files to see what data the attacker was stealing.

Back in the CAT, the biggest question is "What did they take?" Unfortunately, you may never know for sure. If the forensics investigation reveals access to certain servers or systems, then you can be reasonably assured that they had access to everything on that particular server. However, if the forensics evidence is inconclusive, then you will have to assume the worst case scenario and pay for credit monitoring protection for every one of your customer's records. But it does not stop there. Other concerns include:

- What do you with many of your employees who can no longer do their job without email, Internet access, or inter-site communications? Do you send them home? With full pay?
- Are there accounts payable that must be paid by a certain date otherwise face late penalties? How do you make these payments?
- If your business has retail locations, do you need to close? Can your Point of Sale systems still connect to merchant banks? What do you do to assure your on-premise customers that everything is OK?
- Can you re-route your online transactions to other sites to maintain your online businesses?

Recovery and Lessons Learned

Recovery may take months for large-scale incidents. However, the focus should have been to increase the overall security with relatively quick (days to weeks) and high value changes to prevent future incidents during the earlier stages of the breach. The later phases should focus on longer-term changes (e.g., major infrastructure or network changes) and ongoing work to keep the enterprise as secure as possible. IT will restore systems to normal operations, confirm systems are functioning how they should, and remediate vulnerabilities to prevent similar incidents. Yet, recovery may involve rebuilding systems from scratch, replacing compromised files with clean versions, installing patches, changing passwords, and tightening network perimeter security. It might be advisable, depending on the maturity of your cyber security program, to maintain your third party Incident Response vendor, or bring in a new IT support vendor to assist with expediting the recovery phase if IT has limited resources.

Once an organization is successfully breached, the same (or other) hackers who know the company is vulnerable often attack it again. We have seen this many times; most recently (December 2015) with Neiman Marcus being breached for a second time in two tears. The CAT should approve immediate procurement of new security technologies that should have already been in place and could possibly have prevented this breach.

One of the most important parts of incident response is learning and improving. Your cyber security program must constantly evolve to reflect new threats, improved technology, and lessons learned. Once things return to normal, your CISO will conduct a detailed "lessons learned" review with all involved parties, as soon after the breach as is feasible (ideally within several days of the end of the incident). This review meeting will achieve closure with respect to the breach by reviewing the events, the successes, and the areas requiring improvements. To this point, the following questions should be considered during a lessons learned review:

- Exactly what happened and what was the full timeline?
- How well did your teams and vendors perform?
- What information did your teams require and how could they have received it sooner?
- What should be done differently in the next incident?
- What precursors or indicators should be watched for in the future to detect similar incidents?
- What additional tools or resources are needed to detect, analyze, and mitigate future incidents?
- What were your weak areas and what are the steps/who is responsible to make the necessary changes?
- Were there any star performers who went above and beyond? How are you going to recognize them? Cash award? Time off award? Both?

For those identified areas that need improvement, a plan of action and milestones should be created with specific tasks listed and assigned to individuals, or teams, with estimated dates of completion. Regular follow-up meetings should be held until each one of these tasks is completed.

The Aftermath

Now that you have survived the breach (and have the financial and reputation scars to prove it), "What's next?" What can you expect over the next 3, 6, and 12 months? What is the best way to dig yourself out of the deep hole in which you may find yourself?

To that end, let's look at some of the things that might still be ongoing.

- **Data Analysis.** Your cyber security team and incident response vendor are most likely still running forensics and analyzing data from all sources to gather all the pieces to complete the picture of exactly what happened, when it happened, and how. This will be important for you later in your reporting to the government, regulators, merchant banks, cyber insurance companies, and in litigation.

- **Litigation.** If you lost PCI and/or PHI information, you can expect to have multiple lawsuits filed against you within days following public announcement of the breach. Often times, a large law firm experienced in prosecuting cyber security breach cases will try to consolidate these cases and file one large class action lawsuit. This actually works in your favor, so that you don't have to duplicate time and expenses litigating multiple cases in multiple jurisdictions, states, and countries for the same issue.

- **Regulatory Issues.** Government agencies who might have some jurisdictional authority over you will build a case against you to determine your negligence and/or failure to perform your due diligence in protecting customer data, and to determine the amount of forthcoming fines.

- **Insurance Investigation.** If you have cyber insurance, your insurer will investigate to determine if they are going to pay out on your claim and, if so, how much.

- **Rebuilding Brand Damage.** Customers have lost confidence in your company and are taking their business to your competitors. How do you rebuild your brand and reputation?

What can you do to help alleviate these issues? Here are a few things to get you going in the right direction:

- **Post-Breach Report.** First, have your CISO provide your legal team with a comprehensive list of the steps you took to build your cyber security program. Include policies, training, strategic plans, new or upgraded tools and technologies, additional cyber personnel hired, anything and everything you can provide to prove that you were going above and beyond industry best practices.

  - **Working with External Counsel.** Engage external counsel experienced in either prosecuting or defending cyber security breach cases. External counsel will have the experience to support you in complex litigation and also have access to bring witnesses who can provide expert testimony showing that you have performed your due diligence and exceeded industry best practices; provided that you actually have. They also have proven and persuasive graphics and other arguments which they can use to support your case.

  - **External Public Relations.** You also might consider hiring an external Public Relations/Media firm experienced in assisting breached businesses. They can significantly help in restoring your organization's brand and reputation damaged by the breach. They also can assist in managing the other regulatory, financial, and legal challenges you will face post-breach. They are experienced in getting the right message out to your customers, merchants, banks, regulators, pundits, shareholders, and others to help you restore your image quicker than trying to stumble through it on your own.

Prior to a breach, it is very useful to maintain a list of the law firms, public relations companies, and other organizations that can assist you if tragedy strikes. In fact, there are many who you can prearrange and execute contingency contracts. No retainer payments are necessary, but maintaining a legal contingency plan will never hurt. When you need them, you make a phone call and then execute the preapproved contracts and Statements of Work. Time is of the essence during a breach, and this will help expedite your recovery.

This chapter provided you with a glimpse of the chaotic events that take place during a cyber security breach. Use the information provided in this chapter and include it in your Incident Response Plan and Program. Take it one step further and ensure your CISO includes it in your periodic Incident Response training. Planning for this event will make you much better prepared for it, and it also will help your organization recover from the carnage much faster. Time is money, so every bit you can save will help to protect the bottom line of your organization.

In the next chapter, we will summarize the key points that we have discussed so far in this book, and provide you with a roadmap for your cyber security program. We also include the perspective of several of my colleagues in Fortune 200 organizations who have built industry leading cyber security programs.

Chapter 8:

Cyber Security Roadmap: *The Path to a Rock Solid Program*

The Cyber Security Roadmap

Congratulations, you've made it this far and now have a much better understanding of why cyber security is so important to the success of your organization. You are also aware of the perils if you don't provide adequate support and resources, both fiscal and human.

Let's recap and summarize the highlights of the journey to this point:

First, the threat is real. The threat of a cyber breach is so high that no organization is safe. If you aren't using cutting edge cyber security technologies, and don't have well-trained personnel operating those technologies, then you very well could be breached already. But how do you know if you are breached? How do you know if you have the right people, processes, and technologies? Please don't look to IT, because remember that cyber security is not an IT function. As a Board Director or C-Suite executive, it is your responsibility to make sure you have the right people, processes, and technologies in good order.

Assessing Your Internal Risk

To properly assess your organization's risk, the first step is to conduct a strategic cyber security risk assessment. To this end, it is advantageous for you to bring in a 3rd party cyber security consultant who is an expert in cyber security risk management frameworks. You cannot build a rock solid program unless you know where to begin. The consultant, or your CISO, should then prepare a Cyber Security Strategic Plan, which indicates your next steps, how often they should be done, and the required and necessary resources. Chapter 1 provides you with the detailed information on what areas need to be included in the strategic cyber security assessment.

Keep in mind that cyber risk is business risk. Everything you do or don't do in cyber security can have a significant impact on shareholder value and the financials of the business.

It Takes a Village to Prevent a Breach

Now that we have the assessment completed and your CISO has a strategic plan to start building your program, your job is done, right? Absolutely not! The threat landscape is constantly evolving. Staying ahead of the attackers is a constant and ongoing battle. For this reason, cyber security must be on the agenda of every board meeting. CEOs must require a regular update from the CISO. Refer to Chapter 2 for a list of questions that you should be asking of your CISO to make sure that you have a clear picture of your risk profile versus security profile.

Each of the C-Suite executives in your organization has very specific cyber security roles and responsibilities in managing the cyber risk of the company. But cyber security is not just an executive function. It takes a village to prevent a breach. From the Board down through the executives to each and every employee in the organization, all parties maintain responsibility in creating a secure culture and doing their due diligence to keep the business safe. This message should be communicated from the top and permeated through the entire organization.

Separating the Real from the Fake

As we saw in the examples in Chapter 3, whether you are an enterprise size organization, or a small to medium size business (SMB), the primary attack vector for many attackers is through spear phishing email. The attackers know that the weakest link in the chain often is individual end users. The attackers are very sophisticated and it is often difficult to detect a well-crafted spear phishing email. Equally as difficult to detect is a drive by download of malware from a compromised web page of a valid business website; particularly an attack that only runs in memory and does not create malware embedded files on the endpoint system. There are technologies to address these major holes, but you must provide your CISO the resources to implement these leading-edge technologies.

If you are an SMB, you might not have the ability to hire a rock star CISO or have a full cyber security team monitoring your networks, but armed with the information in this book you can better define the requirements for your external Managed Security Services Provider (MSSP). Do not develop a false sense of security thinking that your MSSP will take care of everything. They will do only what you pay them to do. You must very clearly define the Statement of Work and tell them exactly what you need, as well as establish proper Service Level Agreements.

Also in Chapter 3 we separated the fact from the fiction surrounding cyber security. We discussed the five biggest myths in cyber security:

- **MYTH #1: We've never been breached, so our security must be good.**
- **MYTH #2: We've invested millions in cyber security, so we will not be breached.**
- **MYTH #3: We're a small company, so we won't be attacked.**
- **MYTH #4: We're 100% compliant, so we must be secure.**
- **MYTH #5: Cyber Security is an IT Function.**

Dispelling these myths provided you with clarity in these areas that will help you to better evaluate and analyze where your focus needs to be with regards to cyber security within your organization.

Understanding the Impact of a Breach

Before we dove into how to build your rock solid cyber security program, in Chapter 4 we took an in depth look at the impact that a cyber security breach can have on your organization. Some of the major impact areas we discussed included:

- **Brand and Reputation Damage**
- **Loss of Intellectual Property**
- **Class Action Lawsuits**
- **Government and Regulatory Fines**
- **Company and Executive Personal Liability**
- **Loss of Shareholder Value**

- **Loss of Current and Future Revenue/Cash Flow**
- **Significant Legal Fees**
- **Executive Dismissals**

It is not a one size fits all set of circumstances, and any one ancillary effect of a breach could lead to total loss. The truth is that a cyber-breach does not impact just one facet of a business. It can literally bring the entire company to its knees.

Creating a Rock-Solid Program

In Chapter 5 we discussed prescriptive measures that are effective, regardless of the size of your organization or the risk level of your particular business and industry. Depending on the size of your business, you can take these resources and then scale the size of your program. There is not a one-size-fits-all solution. Each business will have unique risks, different threats and vulnerabilities, and specific levels of risk tolerance. An extensive list prioritizing your cyber security investments to maximize each dollar spent was included in this chapter. How you implement these guidelines will vary. But ultimately, it is designed to help you better reduce and manage the cyber security threats faced by your business.

Now it's time to actually build your program. Where do we start? What are the first steps we should take before we actually implement or upgrade the organized structure of our cyber security program? The following steps will answer those questions and begin your journey to create a rock solid cyber security program:

- **Make a Decision!**
- **Hire a Rock Star CISO**
- **Conduct a Strategic Cyber Security Assessment**
- **Budget Fiscal Resources**
- **Managing the Human Element**
- **Insource or Outsource Security**
- **Building and Organizing the Cyber Security Team**

We also discussed one of the more challenging areas of building your team, and that is with the hiring process and the hiring of your rock star CISO, managerial experts, and your cyber security Subject Matter Experts. These team members will lead and compose the major areas of responsibility of the cyber security program, which include:

- **Monitoring**

- **Incident Response**

- **Security Architecture & Engineering**

- **Compliance and Governance**

- **Policy & Training**

- **Project Management**

It is important to note the connection between cyber security and the role it plays in your overall organization. A key component of any rock solid cyber security program is integration with your business. Effectively folding cyber security into business processes allows your executive management team to make better risk management decisions on business investments and operations.

The Role and Responsibilities of a CISO

In Chapter 6 we focused on your rock star CISO. The CISO is the C-level executive responsible for cyber security within your organization. The CISO should report to the CEO to be most effective to the business. Although the CISO is typically identified closely with Information Technology (IT), the CISO's cyber security organization is fundamentally different than IT. The IT department is primarily responsible for the operation and maintenance of the organization's networks, systems, applications, technology development, and communications systems. They provide technological solutions for the business, but they are not a security organization. It is the CISO's responsibility to then make sure the level of risk is aligned to the risk appetite of the business, as determined by the board and executive leadership.

We defined the qualities and characteristics of a rock star CISO including:

- **Leadership**
- **Strategic Thinker**
- **Great Communicator**
- **Technologist**
- **Expert Crisis Manager**
- **Team Builder**
- **Problem Solver**

We also discussed in depth the major responsibilities of the CISO, including:

- **Security Assessments**
- **Risk Management**
- **Policy and Governance**
- **Security Architecture and Engineering**
- **Security Monitoring**
- **Incident Response**
- **Cyber Threat Intelligence**
- **Forensics**

We also discussed the financial management of cyber risks and the value of having cyber risk insurance; what it covers, what it doesn't, and exclusions to be aware of.

Recovering from the Carnage

Chapter 7 described a real world example of something you are trying to avoid – a cyber breach. To survive a data breach, and potential post-breach litigation, organizations must have a two-part Incident Response Program:

- The technical response handled by the CISO and his cyber security teams and
- A well-planned and executed crisis management solution.

During a major breach, an effective program will bring order to a chaotic environment. And chaos there will be. We took you through the chaos of a breach and looked specifically at the roles and responsibilities of

C-Suite executives during a breach. We took you through the containment, mitigation, and recovery from the breach. Also, one of the most important parts of incident response is learning and improving. Your cyber security program must constantly evolve to reflect new threats, improved technology, and lessons learned. Once things return to normal, your CISO will conduct a detailed "lessons learned" review with all involved parties, as soon after the breach as is feasible.

And finally we took a close look at the aftermath of a breach to prepare you for what you can expect over the next 3, 6, and 12 months post-breach to help you figure out the best way to dig yourself out of the deep hole in which you may find yourself.

Regardless of the situation, it is through experts and industry specialists that we not only create strong infrastructure, but also execute a responsive game plan if the need arises. To that end, we will spend the remainder of the book discussing cyber security with industry leaders and experts to better understand what occurs every day in the trenches.

The Experts Roundtable

What you have read thus far is not just my personal opinions or ideas. These are tried and true principles developed over years in the federal government and Fortune 500 organizations. To support these ideas, I have reached out to a few of my colleagues and some of the top CISOs in the country to ask their thoughts on the most important aspects of building a rock solid cyber security program. Here are their responses:

Mr. Bruce Brody

Mr. Bruce Brody is the former CISO for two of the largest US government agencies – the US Department of Veterans Affairs and the US Department of Energy. Brody also has served as a CISO in multiple Fortune 500 companies, and currently is a Director of Cyber Security for PricewaterhouseCoopers in Washington DC. Earlier, Brody told me "The CISO has an organizational transformation role, with strong hooks into IT, Risk, HR, GC, Physical Security and the entire enterprise, top to bottom. Creating a risk-conscious and security-aware culture across the enterprise should be the first priority of a CISO. Maintaining a risk-conscious and security-aware culture across the enterprise should be the second priority of a CISO."

I asked Brody his response if he had a conversation with a CEO and was asked what five things must be done to provide adequate security for our enterprise. Brody replied, "Let me start by saying that these five things are just the beginning. It doesn't mean the enterprise will be secure once you have these five things, but if we don't start with these five things, we'll never have a prayer at securing your enterprise. And we have to know these five things at all times and with 100% certainty. Unfortunately, most enterprises don't know these five things right now, and they are ripe for attacking and breaching.

"First, we have to know with 100% certainty at all times what are the boundaries of our interconnected enterprise, including all network topologies, including all wireless and remote connections, including any cloud computing. What is the boundary of the enterprise within which all of your business is being conducted today?

"Second, we have to know the devices, all of them, that are connected to your interconnected enterprise, at all times, and with 100% certainty.

"Third, we have to know what are the configurations of those devices, with 100% certainty at all times.

"Fourth, we have to know who is accessing those devices, with 100% certainty at all times.

"And fifth, we have to know what these people are doing when they're accessing these devices.

"I realize I just hit you with everything from device discovery to configuration management to identity management to continuous monitoring, with a whole lot of excursions in between. But I will tell you that if we don't know these five things with 100% certainty at all times, we can't manage the risk in our enterprise.

"Remember, this is just where we start."

Take moment to think about Brody's comments. There is a lot to think about as you and your CISO are building your rock solid cyber security program. You know what your crown jewels are and where they are located (give yourself a hand as many organizations don't know where the crown jewels are), but now you have to know all the areas Brody mentions in order to protect the crown jewels. A daunting task for even the most seasoned security professionals!

Mr. Lou DeSorbo

Lou DeSorbo is the CISO for Health Net, a $14B Fortune 200 organization. DeSorbo is responsible for developing, implementing, and operating all information and physical security capabilities across the portfolio of Health Net's enterprise while ensuring all physical and technological environments are appropriately secured and comply with applicable regulatory, contractual, and compliance requirements. Day to day, he leads the cyber security operations, cyber risk and compliance, corporate security, and transportation security teams. Previously, DeSorbo served in a variety of senior leadership roles with the federal government and the Department of Defense.

DeSorbo was asked what he thinks are the most important aspects in building an industry leading cyber security program. He stated:

"First, which unfortunately is not always a given, you must have the complete support of the organization's executive leadership. Without leadership's support you cannot build a great program.

"Second, you must have a repeatable and measurable framework such as the NIST Cyber Security Risk Management Framework. This is the foundation of your program – Identify, Protect, Detect, Respond, and Recover. We really need to get much better at performing these five basic tasks.

"Third, we need outstanding leaders. Leaders take care of people and people take care of the mission. We need more leaders who can take action and improve the capabilities of our people, processes, and technology.

"Fourth, I make sure I have the right motivated, passionate people. If they are passionate but not trained, then my job is to train them and hold them accountable. We have too many 'C' players but not enough 'A' players. Unfortunately, unless you have operated at the 'A' level, you don't know what it is. So we have to give them training and direction to be successful.

"Finally, cyber risk is business risk. It's about realizing you will never have perfect security. We must engage with the business about identifying acceptable levels of risk and manage that rather than focusing just on technology. Identify risk stakeholders, work with the right groups and get them to understand the risk portfolio, and help them manage the daily risk decisions."

Mr. Malcolm Harkins

Malcolm Harkins is the Global Chief Information Security officer (CISO) at Cylance Inc. He is responsible for all aspects of the company's information risk and security, public policy, and for outreach to help improve understanding of cyber risks and best practices for managing and mitigating them. Harkins previously served 23 years with Intel, as its first Chief Security & Privacy Officer (CSPO). In that role he was responsible for managing the risk, controls, privacy, security, and other related compliance for Intel along with all of its products and services.

Harkins was a contributing author to IT Privacy: A Handbook for Technologists, published by the International Association of Privacy Professionals (2014). In 2012 he published his first book, Managing Risk and Information Security: Protect to Enable. He regularly speaks at leading cyber security events and writes articles and white papers.

Harkins was asked to describe the steps we should take to create strong, protective barrier within our organizations. He stated:

"We need security champions and equally heroic security solutions. Boards and corporate executives are committed to bolstering cyber defenses. Yet these desires, and even increased budgets, won't help them fend off attackers unless they move beyond the doom-and-gloom mentality that is rampant across the security industry. While showing companies how simple cyber-attacks can be is a powerful 'ah-ha' moment for many, some vendors take it too far, extending that fear broadly as a marketing tool. Unfortunately, scaring people into buying products has done little to make the world more secure.

"We as an industry need to do more to position CISOs, CSOs, CPOs and their senior staff to win the cyber battles by empowering them to rethink budgets, eliminate bureaucracy, and work to change corporate cultures and behaviors. They need acumen in business and a deep understanding of technology along with more specialized expertise in risk, security, and controls. Those that excel in these practice areas will be seen as heroes and heroines in their organization.

"We need to openly discuss what it takes to be a heroic security professional, exploring how to succeed in navigating these challenges. We need leaders to demonstrate character and integrity in taking a stand on tough issues with no air cover. They will often be required to make difficult, independent decisions and take responsibility for outcomes. As General George Marshall once said, 'It is not enough to fight. It is the spirit which we bring to the fight that decides the issue.'

"Heroes and heroines can't win battles alone, so they must learn how to communicate, coordinate, and convince others to take action. They also need to try new approaches; driving teams to approach risk much like firefighters would assess a blaze – looking to protect their organization's people and property by running towards the risk, not away.

"Over the years I have witnessed many in the security community demonstrate heroic qualities. Peers have shared sensitive details about intrusions at their organizations so that others could protect themselves. Others have chosen to embrace cloud, mobility, and social computing, accepting accountability for dealing with new risks to avoid constraining innovation and productivity at their businesses. And there are those who take the lonely path of challenging the business to do better to protect customer privacy. I admire those people because they are courageous and do not act out of fear. They act out of purpose to protect in order to enable people, data, and business.

"As professionals, we must strive to be heroes and heroines, accept responsibility to implement change, and be accountable for results. As vendors we need to produce heroic products that lower risk, cut costs, and improve user experience."

Mr. Jay Leek

Since May of 2012, Jay Leek has been a Managing Director and the Chief Information Security Officer (CISO) for Blackstone. He oversees the Blackstone Portfolio Company Information Risk & Security Community. Prior to joining Blackstone, Jay established, built, and headed up global information risk and security programs for Equifax and Nokia. Over the past 20 years he worked as a product manager as well as a consultant to numerous telecom companies, government agencies, and financial institutions assisting them with business development, strategic planning, and architectural design required to meet their information risk and security objectives.

When asked about the most important component of building an effective, industry leading cyber security program, he stated, "From Day 1 the big focus must be on education, education, education of C-Suite execs and Board Directors. I don't go into the details or specifics of the technical security plans, but focus more on educating them on who the threat actors are, where attacks are coming from, why they are being attacked, the difference between cyber crime and cyber espionage, and how does knowing the attack location change the response. I keep the education at a high level and keep it focused on a business related perspective.

"The executives must understand the impact that attacks from Advanced Persistent Threats and other Nation States can have on the business and our customers. These senior executives must believe that one of the most significant, if not THE most significant, threat or risk to the company is a cyber attack. Once they have this level of understanding they become more inquisitive and start talking to their peers in other companies and the government about cyber threats. They start to believe that it's not IF but WHEN. This level of understanding then translates into their complete support in building a comprehensive cyber security program. CEOs should identify a cyber security leader in their organization. They need to have an executive leader who is dedicated solely to cyber security. Second, they must meet quarterly with that cyber security leader face to face. They also should communicate outside those quarterly meetings, ask questions, and make sure that the cyber leader can effectively communicate in terms that they clearly understand."

These industry experts should give you at least a 20,000-foot glimpse into those areas of industry interest. They are the captains in the battle against cyber-threats and their insight and knowledge is unbelievably valuable, especially in the beginning of your growth as a company. Take special note of their suggestions and use them as building blocks for a thoughtful and purposeful cyber security program.

A Cyber Farewell

The goal of this book was to help you gain an in depth understanding of each of these significant areas while learning exactly what steps you, as a leader, can take to properly prepare your organization to face today's constantly evolving threat landscape.

Remember: never become complacent about cyber security. We have seen cases where some C-level executives are confident that their security is very good and are not concerned about a forthcoming breach. This type of thinking should be cause for serious alarm. When international security company RSA was breached, they too thought they had very tight security. In fact, they did have excellent perimeter security and detection capabilities. They probably thought their own security was very tight because they were a very well-known and respected company built around marketing security products to keep other companies secure. Unfortunately, that thinking cost them $66 million, not including the cost of brand and reputation damage.

In that breach the attacker knew RSA had good perimeter security and monitored their systems closely. So the attacker researched and found some of RSA's 3rd party business partners. They successfully breached a partner's systems, who had weaker security, then sent email from that company to RSA employees with an Excel spreadsheet attached that contained malware. Interestingly, the email actually went into a spam folder, yet the RSA employee pulled it out of the spam folder and opened the Excel spreadsheet and compromised RSA and their network.

However, the story doesn't end there. RSA, too, was a pivot point for the attacker to get to its real target that was Lockheed Martin, one of the world's largest defense contractors. This just proves that malicious actors will go multiple levels down a supply chain to reach its intended victim. How well are you performing 3rd party vendor oversight and management? So even when you build your rock solid program following the information presented in earlier chapters, always remember that the attackers are going to look for every little crack in the armor and then attack it.

Hopefully, you have gained a much better understanding of the cyber security threats targeting your business and your industry, as well as assessing why these big companies are getting breached. Next, evaluate what you can do to significantly lower your risk and raise your security so as not to become a victim, and then recognize what you must do as a senior executive to implement a comprehensive cyber security program. Finally, starting your plan immediately will likely position you to dodge the full impact and financial effects of a breach, as well as the damage it can cause to organizations. But even then, if a breach occurs, you should be ready to determine the necessary steps to manage a cyber security crisis.

So right now, right when you close this book, here are five steps you should take to improve your cyber security:

1. Make the decision to build a rock solid cyber security program and take action.

2. Hire an external consultant to conduct a strategic cyber security assessment of your organization so you know exactly what your risk profile looks like.

3. Update the strategic goals of the organization to include cyber security as a top priority to make it clear to every person in the company that you are serious about preventing a cyber breach and the subsequent egregious damage it will cause.

4. Allocate sufficient fiscal resources to the CISO and the authorization to right size the staffing, as you need to immediately invest in the people, processes, and technologies to keep your business safe.

5. Communicate to the entire organization that cyber security is a top priority, and that all employees must practice sound cyber security in all their daily activities.

We now live in a world with cyber-threats around every corner. Even one data breach can be unrecoverable to your business. But preventative maintenance is not nearly as difficult as you think. Investing a little bit of time and money now can be the difference between success and ultimate demise. So together we can overcome the new generation of thieves who can literally rob you blind while wearing their pajamas and sitting in front of their computers.

Finally, you now have access to one of the top cyber security experts in this country who can assist you in developing your strategic plan and goals for protecting your organization. Feel free to reach out to me through my website or by email to schedule a rewarding call.

ABOUT THE AUTHOR

Mr. Phillip J. Ferraro
Global Chief Information Security Officer
Best Selling Author
International Keynote Speaker

Mr. Phillip J. Ferraro is an advisor to C-Suite executives and board level directors. He provides extensive and demonstrated knowledge on cyber security risk management, develops and implements world-class cyber security programs designed to protect and defend against the world's most sophisticated attackers, and ensure compliance with multiple regulatory standards.

Mr. Ferraro was recognized in October 2014 with the Evanta Top Ten CISO Breakaway Leader Award. He also is one of the few CISOs in the country who has presented on Capitol Hill on cyber security and advanced threats to Senate and Congressional Committees.

Mr. Ferraro served as the Vice President and Global Chief Information Security Officer for the Las Vegas Sands Corp, a Fortune 200 organization. In his role as Global CISO, he designed and built all aspects of the global Cyber Security program including strategic planning and business alignment, global cyber security operations, threat intelligence, security architecture and engineering, as well as PCI, SOX, and gaming compliance.

Prior to this, Mr. Ferraro was the CISO for DRS Technologies, a $10B Cleared Defense Contractor, where he was responsible for strategic and tactical planning, and compliance with the Defense Security Service national security protection requirements. He was instrumental in deploying cutting edge cyber security technologies focusing on prevention over detection and response.

Mr. Ferraro served the US Federal government for 30 years including positions as the CISO for the Federal Communications Commission (FCC), and similar roles with the Department of Defense for the United States Army, Europe, and the United States Southern Command in Miami, Florida. In these roles, he was instrumental in revitalizing the cyber security programs and significantly increased the overall security posture, and became a subject matter expert in cyber espionage and battling advanced persistent threats.

Mr. Ferraro also served in the U.S. Army with a distinguished career in U.S. Army Special Forces (Green Berets). Throughout his Special Operations career he served numerous overseas tours in Southeast Asia, Central and South America, and Southwest Asia.

Mr. Ferraro holds a Master's Degree in Information Technology from City University of Seattle. His many Information Technology industry certifications include Certified Information Systems Security Professional (CISSP), Certified Information Security Manager (CISM), Certified Ethical Hacker (CEH), Cisco Certified Network Associate (CCNA), Checkpoint Certified Security Engineer (CCSE), Microsoft Certified Security Engineer (MCSE), and several others.

He can be reached through his website at www.phillipferraro.com

CPSIA information can be obtained
at www.ICGtesting.com
Printed in the USA
LVOW10*1159120617
537815LV00022B/989/P